# Vellenaux

## A Novel

E. W. Forrest

**Alpha Editions**

This edition published in 2024

ISBN : 9789362921390

Design and Setting By
**Alpha Editions**
www.alphaedis.com
Email - info@alphaedis.com

As per information held with us this book is in Public Domain.
This book is a reproduction of an important historical work. Alpha Editions uses the best technology to reproduce historical work in the same manner it was first published to preserve its original nature. Any marks or number seen are left intentionally to preserve its true form.

# Contents

PREFACE ............................................................................- 1 -
CHAPTER I. ........................................................................- 2 -
CHAPTER II. .....................................................................- 10 -
CHAPTER III. ...................................................................- 17 -
CHAPTER IV. ...................................................................- 24 -
CHAPTER V. .....................................................................- 32 -
CHAPTER VI. ...................................................................- 42 -
CHAPTER VII. ..................................................................- 51 -
CHAPTER VIII. .................................................................- 60 -
CHAPTER IX. ...................................................................- 67 -
CHAPTER X. ....................................................................- 75 -
CHAPTER XI. ...................................................................- 83 -
CHAPTER XII. ..................................................................- 90 -
CHAPTER XIII. .................................................................- 96 -
CHAPTER XIV. ...............................................................- 103 -
CHAPTER XV. ................................................................- 112 -
CHAPTER XVI. ...............................................................- 118 -
CHAPTER XVII. ..............................................................- 125 -
CHAPTER XVIII. .............................................................- 133 -
CHAPTER XIX. ...............................................................- 136 -
CHAPTER XX. ................................................................- 143 -
CHAPTER THE LAST. .....................................................- 151 -

# PREFACE

The consideration and favor accorded to the writer's former works by a generous reading public, has induced him to try his hand as a novelist, and the present effort "Vellenaux" is the result.

The Book, although essentially one of fiction, contains many episodes of an historical character. In fact, truth and imagination are so blended together, that the reader will scarcely discover where the one begins or the other ends. Scenes and occurrences are portrayed which took place during the Sheik Wars, the siege of Mooltan, the battle of Chillianwalla, and the never to be forgotten Sepoy Mutiny, with the simple alteration of names, dates and localities. On the shoulders of the hero has been grafted many of the adventures, exploits and escapes which in reality occurred either to the Author himself or some of his many military acquaintances, in doing which the reader may rest assured that no character or incident has been in any way overdrawn.

**THE AUTHOR.**

# CHAPTER I.

The bright rays of an Autumn sun fell upon the richly stained glass, sending a flood of soft, mellow rainbow tinted light through the quaintly curved and deeply mullioned windows which adorned a portion of the eastern wing of that grand old Baronial residence, Vellenaux, on a fine September morning, at the period during which our story opens. This handsome pile, now the property of Sir Jasper Coleman, had been erected by one of his ancestors, Reginald De Coleman, during the reign of the fifth Henry.

This gallant Knight had rendered that Monarch great service during his wars in France, especially at Agincourt, where his skill and bravery was so conspicuous, and used to so great advantage, that King Henry, on his return to England, rewarded his faithful follower with a grant of land in Devonshire, on which he was enabled, with the spoils he had acquired and the ransoms received from his French prisoners of note, to erect a magnificent chateaux, which he called Vellenaux, after Francois, Count De Vellenaux, a French noble, whose ransom contributed largely to its construction. Here he continued to reside until his death, which occurred several years after.

It was now an irregular edifice, having been partially destroyed and otherwise defaced during the contests which ensued between the cavaliers and roundheads at the time of the Commonwealth. Since then alterations and additions had been made by his successors, and, although of different styles of architecture, was now one of the handsomest and most picturesque structures that could be met with throughout the length and breadth of the shire.

A broad avenue of noble elms led from the lodge at the entrance of the domain and opened upon a beautiful carriage drive that wound round the velvet lawn, which formed a magnificent and spacious oval in front of the grand entrance.

Beneath the outspreading branches of the venerable oaks, with which the home park was studded, browsed the red and fallow deer, who, on the approach of any equestrian parties, or at the advance of some aristocratic vehicle bearing its freight of gay, laughing guests towards the hospitable mansion, would toss their antlered heads, or, startled, seek the cover of those green shady alleys leading to the beech woods which adjoined the park and stretched away towards the coast of Devon.

Sir Jasper, who was still a bachelor, and on the shady side of sixty, retained much of the fire and energy of his earlier years, although at times subject to an infirmity which the medical faculty describe as emanating from disease of the heart. He had served with great distinction during the Peninsular war, under the iron Duke, but, on succeeding to the Baronetcy, left the service and retired to his present estate, where he spent most of his time at this his favorite residence, as hunting, shooting and field sports generally had for him a charm that no allurements of city life could tempt him to forego; besides he had, in the earlier part of his military career, visited many of the gay capitals of Europe and engaged in the exciting pleasures always to be met with in such places, until he had become satiated and lost all taste for such scenes. His kind heartedness and benevolence won for him the esteem of the neighboring gentry.

On the morning in question the Baronet, who had but the evening previous returned from London, entered his study, and seating himself in an easy chair, drew towards him a small but elaborately carved antique escritoire, and for several moments was deeply engaged in the perusal of certain papers and memoranda; finally he drew from his pocket a sealed packet which, having opened carefully, he read over; then as if not quite satisfied with the contents, allowed the paper to slip from his hand to the table before him and was soon lost in thought. An English gentleman, unquestionably in the highest sense of the word, was Sir Jasper Coleman; a true type of that class who, from the time of the Norman conquest to the present day, whether beneath the Torrid or Frigid Zone's; on the bloody battlefield, or launching their thunders on the billows of the white-crested main, nobly upheld the honor of their country's flag, whose heroic deeds and honorable names have been handed down unsullied and untarnished for many generations. Since leaving the service the worthy Baronet had taken no part in the political events of the nation, but devoted himself entirely to the welfare of his numerous tenantry, and those residing in the neighborhood of his large estate, to whom assistance and advice was at all times needed, nor was it ever withheld or given grudgingly when any case of real distress came under his notice.

A fine subject fog poet's pen or artist's pencil was that aristocratic old warrior, as he sat there gazing upon the rich woodlands warmed by the glorious autumn sun, thinking over by-gone days—days when he had loitered by some fair one's side in many a brilliant assembly, or when his nerves were steady and his voice all powerful, leading the charge on many a well-fought field. How long he might have remained ruminating on things of the past it is impossible to say; the retrospect might have continued much longer had not his attention been arrested by a slight noise, when suddenly raising his head a smile of pleasure lit up his finely cut features as the door opened and a lovely girl, just merging into womanhood, stepped softly into the room. She was, indeed, very beautiful; hair of the darkest shade of brown hung in long and glossy curls from her perfectly shaped head, and rested on the exquisite white neck and shoulders, the contrast of which showed to a great degree the almost alabaster whiteness of her skin; grecian nose, and eyes of the deepest blue, whose long lashes, when veiled, rested lovingly on her damask cheek, and when raised, revealed a depth and brilliancy which does not often fall to the lot of mortals; a mouth not too small, whose beautifully shaped lips, when parted, disclosed to the beholder teeth of ivory whiteness, small and most evenly set, dazzling indeed was the effect of those pearly treasures; tall, slight, and elegantly formed, with a bearing aristocratic and queenly in the extreme; what wonder that she was the sunshine of old Sir Jasper's declining days and his much and dearly loved niece.

Gliding up to her uncle she threw heir arms about his neck and imprinted a kiss on his noble brow, then sinking on a stool at his feet began to take him to task after the following fashion: "You truant, you naughty uncle, to let me breakfast alone in my own room thinking you hundreds of miles away, and not to let me know that you returned last night; and Mrs. Fraudhurst is just as bad, and I will not forgive her or you, unless you tell me where you have been and all you have seen and done. Now, Sir Wanderer, commence and give an account of yourself; you see I am prepared to listen," apparently waiting with much attention for her uncle to enlighten her as to the why and wherefore he had journeyed to London. It was evident that the Baronet had been in the habit of making a confidant of his pretty niece, but on this occasion, for one reason or another he had failed to do so; she had taken out of one of her little embroidered pockets in her apron, some crochet work, and applied herself diligently thereunto.

Edith was the orphan child of Sir Jasper's much loved and only sister, who did not long survive the death of her husband, and on her decease the Baronet had adopted the child, and as she grew up, her affectionate disposition and natural simplicity wound themselves round the old man's heart, and thus she soon became the apple of his eye, and he loved her with all the tender solicitude of a father.

She was gentle and friendly to those beneath her, but dignified and firm with those of her own station of life, with a fund of good practical common sense, and was not easily dissuaded from doing any thing when she had once made up her mind that it was her duty so to do. She loved her uncle well and was ever ready to minister to his slightest wishes. She used to delight him with the rich tone of her voice by singing selections from his favorite operas, being an accomplished musician both vocal and instrumental. They would frequently wander for hours through the park or woods, but of late he had restricted his walks to the lawn, or down the avenue to the lodge at the park gate, to hold converse with the keeper, an old soldier who had served under him in his Peninsular Campaigns, and often when relieved from the attendance on him would Edith and Arthur Carlton, hand in hand, stroll down the said avenue to listen to the wonderful stories related by the old lodge keeper. But this was some time ago, for this youth (of which more will be heard anon) was now, and had been for some time, at College at Oxford.

"Edith my darling," said the kind old man, bending over as he did so and tapping her soft rosy cheek, "my visit to London was purely a business one, and I delayed no longer than was necessary to complete it, but what I saw and heard during my journey to and fro, I will relate to, you in the evening."

The lively girl was about to make some reply to her good natured uncle when a light rapping was heard; the door gently opened and a lady about five and thirty entered; she was attired in a dress of black silk of most undeniable Paris cut, which fitted her to a miracle; to Edith she made a slight inclination of the head so as not to disarrange her coiffure which was most elaborately got up doubtless with a view to produce an effect.

"I trust, Sir Jasper, you slept well after your tedious journey."

"Very well, I thank you. Oh! I see you have the post bag, I am somewhat anxious about some letters I expect to receive."

Moving around the back of the Baronet's chair she came between him and Edith, who took the bag from her and held out her hand to her uncle for the key to open it with, as was her usual custom of a morning; the key was handed to her, and while they were thus engaged the eagle eye of the lady in black fell upon the will which was still lying partially exposed on the escritoire just as it had fallen from Sir Jasper's hand ere he had sank into that reverie which had been disturbed by the entrance of Edith; she obtained but a hurried glance, yet it was sufficient for her to decipher its full meaning. As she realized this a dark cloud passed across her features, she moved silently to the window and looked out; when she again turned the cloud had vanished and her face was calm and serene. So occupied with the mail bag had been both uncle and niece that the action of the lady in question, in first glancing over the paper on the desk and her subsequent movement towards the window, had remained unnoticed by either.

"There is a letter for you, my dear," said the Baronet handing one to Edith. "Oh!" said she joyously, "it is from Arthur. He is the dearest old fellow, and one of the best correspondents alive; he tells the funniest stories of the college scrapes he gets into, and how cleverly he gets out of them, and makes all manner of fun in his caricatures of the musty old professors."

"There, there now, away to your own room," said her uncle, "and let me know what new scrape your dear old fellow has been getting in and out of, during our walk after dinner." Edith blushed slightly and hurried out of the apartment.

"There are no letters for you this morning, Mrs. Fraudhurst, but here are the London papers, I have no time at present to look over them, and would feel obliged if you would lay them on the library table." She took them, and with a graceful courtesy, smilingly left the room, and went direct to the library, sat down at the table and drew the writing materials towards her as if about to write; but ere she commenced her head sank on her hand and she appeared to be, for some moments, lost in thought. As she will be brought prominently forward as our story progresses, we had better inform the reader at once, all we know of her antecedents.

Mr. Fraudhurst had been a lawyer of some standing in the village of Vellenaux; he was reported wealthy, and when on the shady side of fifty married the niece of his housekeeper, much to the disgust of the said housekeeper, and several maiden ladies of doubtful ages who resided in the neighbourhood, who had each in her own mind marked him as her especial property, to be gobbled up at the first opportunity he or chance might afford them for so doing, and they waxed wrath and were very bitter against her who had secured the prize and carried it off when as they thought it just within their grasp. The lawyer and the Baronet had been upon terms of intimacy for several years prior to the marriage, and Sir Jasper being a bachelor saw no objection to his friend's wife visiting Vellenaux, although she had, as he would facetiously observe, risen from the ranks.

The lady in question was, at eighteen, tall, pretty and ambitious. She had at an early age determined to rise above the station in which she was born, and for that object she had studied most assiduously at the village school, where she attained the reputation of being the most apt scholar of her class. A few years residence with a relative London served to develop her natural abilities, and she lost no opportunity of pursuing her studies or of affecting the tone and fashion of persons moving in a far higher circle than her own.

Education and application she knew would doubtless do much to elevate her in the social scale, but the position she so earnestly sought for was to become the wife of some man of good standing in society, whose means would be sufficient to support her in that style to which her ambition led her to hope for, and for this she strove hard and was rewarded for her perseverance by becoming the wife of a reputed wealthy barrister some thirty years her senior, and for a few years enjoying the position she had attained, visiting and visited by the uppercrusts of the place and not unfrequently dining at Vellenaux and otherwise enjoying the hospitality of its owner.

When little Edith was about seven years old, Mr. Fraudhurst was gathered to his fathers, and the sorrowing widow was left in a very different position than was anticipated either by herself or others who took any interest in such matters; the house and grounds which she fully believed to be her own property, passed into the hands of a distant relative of the deceased barrister, and with the exception of the furniture and some three hundred pounds in cash, she was no better off than she had been prior to her marriage; but, being a woman of great tact, she contrived to keep this circumstance from the knowledge of the enquiring neighbours, and having applied to the new owner of the premises she obtained permission to occupy them for a period of six months.

On the Baronet calling to pay his visit of condolence the lady, who had previously arranged what she should say and do on the occasion, unfolded to Sir Jasper her real position and out of friendship for her late husband claimed his advice and assistance. The worthy old bachelor declared his willingness to assist her if she could only point out the way; as to advice he could realty give none on so difficult a matter.

"Oh! Sir Jasper," exclaimed the widow, in a voice so excellently modulated to suit the occasion, that the old bachelor was beginning to feel a real interest in her affairs, "so like yourself, so good of you to allow me to suggest the way in which you can best serve me in my peculiar and, I may say, awkward position."

"There is a way, my dear Sir Jasper, (and here the widow bent over and placed her soft white hand on his arm) in which I believe you can materially serve me, and at the same time advance the interest of one who is, without doubt, more dear to you than any living being; I allude to dear little Edith." At the mention of his niece's name he looked up enquiringly as if not quite catching the meaning of her words.

"You must understand, Sir Jasper," she continued, "that the little darling is now of an age that will require some person to guide and direct the development of her young mind and superintend her studies. Of course, old nurse Simms is an excellent and worthy woman, but not such an one as the future heiress of Vellenaux should be entrusted to, as she advances from childhood to maturity. It is an important and responsible position, and should only be undertaken by those who have already passed through the struggles and trials of the world, and drank of the cup of affliction." Here a pearly tear fell upon the hand of the good-natured Baronet, and here she applied her white laced cambric to her eyes.

This was the *coup de main* that carried the day. The soft-hearted bachelor was not proof against this, besides there was truth and reason in her suggestions for his darling little niece, and he did not see how he could, for the present, do better than to offer to Mrs. Fraudhurst the charge of Edith, and before he took leave it was arranged that the widow should call at Vellenaux daily and endeavor to gain the confidence of the child, and at the end of the six months she should give up housekeeping and be installed as governess and companion for Edith; and so well did she play her cards that she had scarcely been there twelve months when she ruled the household as though she were its legitimate mistress; always heading the table when Sir Jasper entertained his bachelor friends, and thus, we may say, for several years lived in clover. Her chief duties consisted in educating Edith and Arthur, which, for several years, was a task which did not require much mental endowment or physical exertion. It was, in fact, more of a pastime than otherwise, and as she always accompanied Edith when visiting the neighboring families, there was but little monotony to complain of.

She had a double object in becoming an inmate of Vellenaux. First, that of securing a comfortable home for several years. But her grand scheme was that of making herself so necessary to the Baronet, that she could, in time, undermine the defences, carry the Citadel by stratagem, and finally become the envied mistress of Vellenaux. But a few months residence under the same roof served to convince her of the fallacy of the project; for there were two grand difficulties that she could not overcome; his strong objection to matrimony, and his affection for his niece. Therefore, the shrewd and cautious widow had to relinquish her attack in that direction; and as Edith advanced towards womanhood, her position became more precarious. There were two events to be dreaded, and in either case she believed her occupation gone, and these were the death of Sir Jasper or Edith's marriage. Her income during the years of her residence with Sir Jasper had been a handsome one, and being at little or no expense, she managed to accumulate a goodly sum at her bankers; but the idea of losing her present abode was to her disagreeable in the extreme, and her busy mind was continually at work to devise how this could be averted, and this was the way matters stood with her on the morning alluded to.

"He is coming home from College next month not again to return, and she loves him, though she may not at present realize the fact, but that knowledge will come, and I fear much too soon. Sir Jasper will not object, and the youth will hardly refuse to accept Vellenaux and twenty thousand a year, although there be an incumbrance in the shape of a wife attached to the bargain. Yes, I see it all, they will marry and I shall be thrown out in the cold unless I have wit enough to prevent it without appearing to interest myself in any way with what ought not to concern me. But Arthur Carlton must not remain here. He must be sent abroad, to America, India, anywhere, it matters not where, so that they be separated, and that ere long." These were the thoughts that chased each other through the active brain of Mrs. Fraudhurst, as she sat alone in the Library. Half an hour had elapsed ere she had quite made up her mind as to what course she should pursue to avoid the impending evil. Then, at length, seeming to grasp the difficulty, she took up her pen and wrote what she thought was likely to transpire at Vellenaux should there be no one sufficiently interested in the matter to prevent the estate (which had been in the Coleman family for several generations) from passing into other hands. This she sent to one whom she had every reason to believe (for she had observed him well) would not scruple to use any means to gain possession of the broad lands of Vellenaux. This letter the cautious widow posted with her own hands, to prevent the possibility of the address being noticed by either Sir Jasper or Edith. The matter being thus satisfactorily arranged, she patiently awaited the developments of the first fruits of the plot against young Carlton.

# CHAPTER II.

It may be remarked, and with a great deal of truth, that the chapters of a novel bear a certain resemblance to those pleasing illusions known as dissolving views, where one scene glides almost imperceptibly into another. The reader has been gazing mentally on woods, landscapes and water in the South of England, when lo! in the twinkling of an eye, the busy haunts of men in the world's great capitol, London, stands unveiled before him. It must, however, be admitted that, so far as scenic effect is concerned, the change is at times less pleasing than the one just fading from view. Yet if we wish to realize the plot of the story, the dark and uncertain shades of the picture should be looked on, from time to time, as they present themselves.

On a door, which stood partially open, in the last of a row of gloomy looking houses situated in one of those dark and narrow paved courts leading from Chancery Lane to Lincoln Inn Field's, was painted in black letters on a white ground—"Ralph Coleman, Attorney-at-Law."

In the ill lit passage to the right was a door that opened into the front office, where, seated at an old-fashioned desk, was a youth, tall, thin and pale, busily engaged engrossing some legal documents. A short, quick step was heard coming up the Court, the handle turned, the door opened, and a man about the middle height with a slight tendency to be corpulent, and about thirty-five years of age, entered. "Are those papers ready," enquired Mr. Coleman of the young clerk, who had ceased writing on the entrance of his employer.

"I am finishing the last one now," was the ready reply.

"Good; and my letters?"

"They are in the usual place, on your desk," answered the youth, re-commencing his work. The Attorney moved away and entered his private office, and seating himself in his old leathern chair, commenced in a methodical way to open and peruse his letters.

Ralph Coleman commenced life with very fair prospects. He came of a good old family and had received a University education, and studied for the Bar very assiduously for three or four years, but on the death of his father he came in for five thousand pounds. He then neglected his profession, and, for a time, led a very fast life in London. When he had run through about half of his money he went abroad, and while there married a lady who had a tolerable fortune. They travelled together over the European Continent, and for several years enjoyed what is termed life.

An accident happened to Mrs. Coleman in Switzerland which resulted in her death. Ralph being again alone in the world, as it were, entered into all the wild dissipations of Vienna and Paris, which ended in his ruin; and he returned to England with only a five pound note between him and beggary. As the cousin and only male relative of Sir Jasper Coleman, he was heir to the Baronetcy but not to the property. This was unentailed, and at the will of the Baronet; but should he die intestate the whole would fall to Ralph.

But the hope of succeeding to the estate banished, or was at least, to a considerable extent, quashed, when he learned that Miss Effingham had been adopted by her uncle, and that likewise he had made a protégé of the son of his old friend Eustace Carlton, and would no doubt eventually make a will in their favor; but so far as he could learn, up to the present time no will had been made. There was a degree of consolation in this; but in the meantime he must live; he therefore resumed his profession, and by energy, and the aid of his aristocratic friends, succeeded in obtaining a tolerable practice.

He was on pretty good terms with his cousin, and usually went down to Devonshire for a few days during the shooting season, and on more than one occasion had Sir Jasper spoken to him of the future career of young Arthur; but the lawyer generally managed to evade the subject by saying there was plenty of time to think about that when the youngster should leave College, and appeared to interest himself very little in the matter, because he did not see in what way the youth's future career could affect him; that Sir Jasper might assist Arthur with his interest, at the outset, and perhaps give him a couple of hundred pounds to help him on in his profession or calling, he did not at all doubt; but beyond this Ralph did not believe the Baronet would assist him.

"Ah!" said the Attorney, as he took up the fourth letter and glanced at the postmark, "from Devonshire, and the handwriting is that of Mrs. Fraudhurst; what can that maneuvering woman have to communicate? but we shall see, we shall see," and at once opened the letter. The contents were evidently not of an agreeable character, for his brow darken and his lips were firmly compressed as he read the long and closely written epistle. At its conclusion he moved for a few seconds uneasily in his chair, then re-folded the letter and placed it carefully in his pocketbook. With his head resting on his hand he remained sometime in deep thought; presently his brow became clear and, turning to his desk, wrote rapidly for the space of an hour.

"Scrubbins," said he, addressing his confidential (and only) clerk, "I am going to Devonshire, but will return the day after to-morrow; you will find your instructions on my desk, and now give me the deeds; and remember, should any one enquire for me tell them I am gone to the country on business, and shall be back the day after to-morrow," and without farther comment, Ralph Coleman passed out of the office.

It was a still, calm night in early autumn, the silvery moon looked down from her deep violet throne amidst the starry heavens; the dull, heavy sound made by the mighty ocean, as its huge waves were dashed upon the sea-beat shore, fell audibly on the ear in the silent night. A light sea breeze swept through the furze bushes that were scattered over the Downs, across which lay the high road leading past the Park.

Bridoon, the old gate keeper, was seated on his wooden settle within the porch of the lodge, smoking a long clay pipe, and occasionally quaffing long draughts of rare old cider. He was just thinking of turning in for the night, when a vehicle stopped, and a voice demanded admittance. As the gates swung open a gig and its occupant passed through and proceeded at a smart pace along the broad avenue towards the mansion.

The clock of the village church was striking ten as Ralph Coleman pulled up at the principal entrance of Vellenaux, and was met in the hall by Reynolds the old butler, and conducted to the room he usually occupied when visiting there during the shooting season.

"Sir Jasper," said the old servant, "has retired for the night, and Miss Effingham is on a visit to the Willows, but Mrs. Fraudhurst is, I believe, still in the drawing room; will you please to step in there until supper is prepared for you." This suited the lawyer exactly, as he wished to have a few minutes conversation with that lady previous to meeting the Baronet, for the letter he had received from Mrs. Fraudhurst was so cautiously worded, that although sufficiently explicit on most points, there were some portions of it which he could not exactly understand, or see in what way he ought to act, but doubtless she would put him right on all matters that were to be brought quietly to the notice of Sir Jasper. While making some addition to his toilet, it occurred to him that she might be only making a cat's paw of him to feather her own nest, but as he could not see clearly how this could be, dismissed the idea from his mind, and shortly after made his bow to the widow.

She rose and received him courteously; apologised for the absence of the host and his niece, supposed he would feel inclined to retire early, as doubtless he would wish to rise at the dawn of day, to avail himself of the excellent shooting which was to be had in the turnip fields, and was altogether very chatty and agreeable; but she in no way alluded to the letter she had written, to him, he was therefore compelled to broach the subject, and before the supper bell rang, a mutual understanding as to what was to be said and done was arrived at between them.

The Baronet and Mr. Coleman breakfasted alone on the following morning. Edith had not returned, and Mrs. Fraudhurst excused herself on the plea of indisposition, but doubtless she had some other motive for absenting herself.

"And you found the birds plentiful, and in good condition," enquired Sir Jasper, as he pushed away his plate, and turned his chair towards the bright, cheerful fire which was blazing in the polished grate, and stooping down to pat a couple of pointers that were crouching comfortably on the hearth rug at his feet.

"Yes, indeed, quite so, I do not remember a season when the partridges have been so plump or in such numbers, but had hoped to have had your company this morning, but perhaps to-morrow."

"So I have heard, but you must really excuse me, it used to be my chief delight to shoot over the grounds and preserves on a fine autumn morning like the present one, but it is too much for me now, and I have given it up, but I like my friends to enjoy it. How long can you stay this time?"

"Only three days; I cannot be absent from town more than that, but it is well worth the journey to shoot over a friends property, even if only for three days."

"Then you must make the most of your time; old Tom the game-keeper will show you the best covers and general shooting ground. I wish you could have remained for a week or two, the young fellows belonging to the neighboring families will be home from school and college, and there will be plenty of popping then, I promise you. Ah! that reminds me that Arthur Carlton has finished his education, and is coming home, and it is not my intention that he should again return to Oxford; and now we are alone and not likely to be disturbed, I wish you would give me your opinion as to what profession or occupation it would be best for him to embark in. I should like to give the youngster a fair start in life. I have given him the education of a gentleman, and I should like him to retain that position."

This was the turn in the conversation the lawyer had been anxiously waiting for, but he seemed in no hurry to take advantage of it; he shifted his position so that the light might not fall on his features, took a pinch of snuff and crossed one knee over the other before he ventured an opinion on the subject.

"I know so very little of the young gentleman," he began, "as scarcely to be able to advise you on a matter of such moment, and have hitherto declined from so doing on that account, but as you so desire it, I will give my opinion on the matter according to the best of my judgment."

"Thank you, thank you, that is all I ask. Then," resumed the lawyer, "the road by which a young man of education can, by perseverance, hope to earn for himself a competency and a good position in the social scale, is that of the church, the navy or in the military service of his country. As for the pulpit, unless the aspirant has a special tendency for it, or some good friend who has a living to bestow, he will hardly realize a sufficient income to support himself as a gentleman; and to send him up to London to study law, or medicine for two or three years would but expose him to the temptations and dissipations of that great city, and it would take years of drudgery before he would be able to obtain a competency. In my opinion the safest and most expeditious way of proceeding is to put him into the army; his commission and outfit is the only outlay, and can be done at once; his position is established, and it only remains with himself to rise in his profession, and you will be relieved from all care and responsibility on his account; but understand me, I do not mean that he should enter one of the regiments, now in England, to loiter his time away at some country quarters or fashionable watering place, to fall into debt, difficulty, love, or some other absurd scrape, but put him into some corps that is now and will be for some years stationed somewhere abroad, India, for instance, for I have been, by competent authorities, informed that there an officer can live comfortably on the pay of his rank.

"If he is abstemious, and takes care of his health, his promotion must ensue without purchase, and that, too, in a few years. It is a prospect that thousands of youngsters would jump at, and one I think that is in every way suitable for him; this Sir Jasper, is all I have to offer on this subject."

This advice of Ralph Coleman's, although given to effect a preconcerted scheme, was so in unison with the Baronet's views, that he could but assent to what had been uttered by Ralph, and the lawyer had the satisfaction of knowing, ere he left the breakfast room, that his suggestions would be carried out to the letter; and prior to his return to London he had another interview with the wily widow, at which he informed her of the arrangement that had been decided upon by the Baronet in regard to Arthur Carlton's future career. "He will," Ralph went on to say, "be thus removed out of harm's way for several years, and perchance may never again cross your path, and I have no doubt while Sir Jasper lives your position will be secure. I have served your turn without benefitting myself in any way."

"Not so," was the lady's reply, "you have but been paving the way for your own advancement. Why not marry Edith, she is aware that the title falls to you, but is ignorant of the fact that her uncle has made her sole heiress, and girls brought up as she has been, will frequently overlook much to gain a title, and become the envied lady of Vellenaux."

"With young Carlton out of the way, and separated, as they will be, for years, any rising passion she may now feel for him will soon die out, and if you make your advances with caution, and be not too precipitate, I have no doubt that you will eventually secure both the lady and the estate, so of the two, I fancy that you have rather the best of the bargain." And after a little more conversation on the subject, this worthy pair parted.

And now let us introduce the youth whose future welfare had been the difficulty about which the widow and Ralph had given themselves so much concern.

A tall, slight, but decidedly handsome youth, between eighteen and nineteen years of age, wearing the Collegiate cap and gown, was pacing somewhat impatiently up and down the quadrangle of St. John's College, evidently expecting the approach of some person whom he was most desirous of seeing. This was Arthur Carlton, the protégé of Sir Jasper Coleman. He was an orphan, having lost both parents 'ere he knew them. His father had been a Peninsular officer and companion-in-arms of the Baronet, who, on the death of his friend, undertook to see to the education and future welfare of the little Arthur. On losing his mother he had been removed under the care of his nurse to Vellenaux, where he had been only a few months, when the little Edith made her appearance on the scene of action, and being nearly of an age they soon became good friends and fond of the society of each other, because of mutual assistance while pursuing their studies together, which they continued to do until young Carlton was by his kind patron sent to school, prior to his going to college at Oxford. Fond of study, he readily acquired knowledge which he stored up to be used hereafter as circumstances might demand; he was aware of his real position, and that his future success in life must chiefly depend upon his own exertions.

His patron in caring for him during his early years, and giving him the benefit of a university education, had, in the young man's opinion, fully carried out the promise made to his father, on his death bed, whether on the completion of his education his benefactor would continue to assist him by using his interest to procure him some suitable position in which he could carve out for himself, a road to name and fame, he knew not, but nevertheless he felt a deep sense of gratitude for what had already been done for him, by his father's old friend. He was becoming restless when the friend expected advanced at a smart pace to meet him, and proved to be Tom Barton, the youngest son of the Bartons of the Willows, a worthy old couple who resided on their own property, the so called Willows which joined the estate of Sir Jasper Coleman. In this family besides daughters there were two sons, the eldest Horace Barton had graduated at St. John's, and subsequently had obtained an appointment in the civil service of the East India Company, and had gone out to Calcutta, where he had now been for several years. Tom, like his brother, had been educated at Oxford, and was now about leaving college to return to his home for a few weeks, prior to his leaving for London, to pursue the profession he had chosen, that of the law.

"Carlton, my dear fellow, you must really excuse me for thus keeping you waiting; I assure you I could not get away a moment sooner. You can easily imagine the sort of thing, leaving the companionship of those whom for years you have been associated with in many a frolic or academical scrape; but to the point; in what way can I serve you?"

Carlton drew forth a sealed packet from the pocket of his gown, which he handed to him, saying as he did so, "you will confer on me a great favor by calling at Vellenaux and giving this packet into the hand of Miss Effingham. I would rather she should receive it when alone, you will manage this for me, will you not?"

"Certainly, most certainly. I perfectly understand, ah you sly dog; after the pretty heiress are you? I admire your choice, and would I think take the field against you, but for my darling cousin Kate, she will not allow me to flirt with any but herself, so I will do my best for you."

Arthur thanked him heartily, and after a few more words the friends parted, one for his home at the Willows, the other for his small room in the college.

Tom Barton kept his promise, and the packet was duly handed to Edith by him, he having met her walking in the home park the very day of his arrival.

# CHAPTER III.

The time for Arthur's leaving College had now arrived. A few brief lines from Sir Jasper, informing him that he was to leave College at the end of this term for good, but in no way hinting what his future position through life might be, with a small note enclosed from Edith, was all that he had heard from Devonshire since his friend, Tom Barton, had left Oxford; but it was evident from the tone of the Baronet's epistle that he expected him to make Vellenaux his home, at least for the present or until some arrangements could be made for his future.

He was now nineteen, nearly six feet in height and possessed an amount of strength and muscular power seldom met with at his age. These had been developed and matured by boat-racing, cricket and athletic exercises, in which he took great delight. He was likewise an ardent lover of field sports. From the old Lodge keeper, who had been a rough rider in Sir Jasper's troop in the light Dragoons through the greater part of the Peninsular Campaign, he acquired the knowledge of how to sit the saddle and ride like a dragoon, likewise the complete management of his horse; nor was the sabre (the favorite weapon of the old soldier) forgotten, and many a clout and bruise did the youth receive before he could satisfy his instructor as to his efficiency. Being of an obliging disposition, the game keepers took a great deal of trouble to make him a first rate shot, and their exertions were not thrown away, and very proud they were at the way in which he brought down his birds.

Surrounded by some half dozen of his most intimate acquaintances, young Carlton was eating his last collegiate breakfast, as he had to leave for Vellenaux that morning by the 8.20 train, the usual toasts and congratulations had been exchanged, and farewell bumpers of champagne drank, when the porter put his head in at the door and announced in a sharp short tone, "times up, cab at the door." A general rush was made in the direction indicated, Arthur jumped into the vehicle, and amid the shouts and cheers of his friends, was quickly rolled over the stones to the railway terminus. Ding, dong, ding, dong, waugh, waugh, puff, puff, and the train moved slowly out of the station, increasing its velocity until it was whirling along at something very like fifty miles an hour. On reaching Switchem, the station nearest to Vellenaux, Arthur found his horse waiting for him, and from the groom he learned that Sir Jasper was anxiously expecting him, for he had that day accompanied by Edith, gone as far as the lodge gate, a distance much greater than he had walked for some time past. This was very satisfactory for Carlton to know, and with a light heart he sprang into the saddle and cantered merrily along the high road, leading to the park gates, within which the happiest years of his youth had been spent; and the welcome he received from all was of such a character as at once to set at rest any misgivings or apprehensions he might have felt on this score.

Sir Jasper was kind, courteous and almost paternal. Edith could scarcely restrain her delight at the idea of again having in that social circle the playfellow of her childhood and one who had ever been to her as a dear brother, a companion and confidant, one from whom she could always obtain sympathy and advice when annoyed with the petty vexations of childhoods fleeting day. Even Mrs. Fraudhurst, always courteous and polite since his exodus from her scholastic charge, was now more affable and condescending than ever to the Baronet's *protégé*; but she could afford to be so, for she well knew that he was about to be swept from her path, for years, perhaps forever.

The conversation during dinner that evening was animated and general; all parties appeared in the best possible spirits, and anxious to render Arthur's return from college an event to be remembered hereafter with feelings of infinite satisfaction. Soon after the removal of the cloth, the ladies retired, leaving our hero and Sir Jasper alone; the latter having finished a glass of fine old crusted port, settled himself comfortably in his easy chair, and thrusting his thumbs in the armholes of his waistcoat, thus addressed his *protégé*.

"Arthur, my boy, you are now, I think, of an age that would warrant you in judging for yourself as to what particular profession or calling you are best suited to pursue, in order to make a successful career through life. Have you ever given this subject a thought? If so, now we are alone, I should like to hear what your views or ideas may be concerning that matter; it is one of great importance, and requires serious consideration."

Now, although Arthur had anticipated that some such enquiry would be made by the Baronet, he was not quite prepared as to the precise answer it would be best for him to make; in fact he was taken a little aback at the suddenness of the question. He had expected that some days would elapse before Sir Jasper would broach the subject, but being of a straightforward and truthful nature, he frankly stated what he thought respecting his future. "Of course," he said, "Sir Jasper, I shall be guided entirely by any suggestions you may kindly offer, for to you I owe everything. The only path that I believe is open to me is that of Law or Medicine; (and since you allow me) I must candidly acknowledge to either of those professions I have an antipathy; but if it is your wish that I should follow either of these, I can assure you that energy and perseverance shall not be wanting on my part to attain a respectable standing in whatever undertaking I embark in."

"Right, Arthur, right; there is nothing like energy and perseverance in whatever situation, we may be placed in, and now listen to me." The Baronet here took another glass of port, and motioned to Arthur to do the same; then continued he, "Law and Physic are both distasteful to me, nor do I think they are at all suitable for you. The Church is almost out of the question, as I have no interest in that quarter, and could be in no way of use to you. You are beyond the age that lads generally enter the navy; but what say you to the army?" Arthur gave a start at this proposal, and a beam of delight—which he could not conceal—lit up his handsome, though somewhat thoughtful face.

"Oh, Sir Jasper," he exclaimed, "it is the very position I most prize, but one that I had not ventured to hope could be realized; it has been the day dream of my youth."

The kind-hearted old Baronet was evidently much pleased at his young friend's reply and enthusiasm. He took another glass of wine, then said: "I promised your father to give you a fair start in life, and I will keep my word. I have already applied to the Horse Guards on your behalf, and have the refusal of a cornetcy in the Light Dragoons. There, there, say nothing; I see you accept it, so that part of the business is settled so far; but the regiment is now in India, and likely to remain there for some years. Have you any objections to leaving England? If so, you are at liberty to withdraw your consent."

"There is no part of the world that I have so great a desire to visit as British India. I have both heard and read a great deal of that extraordinary country. Besides, is it not the land of my birth?" was Arthur's immediate reply.

"Then consider the matter settled. You will not be required to join your regiment until six months after your name appears in the Gazette. I will write to headquarters and likewise see to your outfit. Of course, you will remain here until after New Year's, and help us to keep up Christmas in the good old English style, for probably it may be the last of the sort you will see for some years; but whatever trials and difficulties you may have to contend with out there, you may rest assured that when the time arrives for you to have your troop, the purchase money shall not be wanting. And now," continued he, as Arthur was about to reply, "send Reynolds to me, I wish to see him on some matters before I retire, and you seek Edith and let her know that you have accepted a commission in the army, as I have not mentioned a word to her concerning it. Please make my excuses to the dear girl for not joining her in the drawing room," then shaking him cordially by the hand, wished him good night.

On entering the drawing room, Arthur found Mrs. Fraudhurst poring over her novel and Edith standing by the French window, looking out upon the Terrace which was now bathed in a flood of pale moonlight. She was wondering what her uncle could have to say to Arthur to detain him so long: she had so much to ask about her ponies and her grayhounds and improvements in her flower gardens, &c. He delivered Sir Jasper's message, then asked her to step out on the Terrace with him. Hastily throwing a mantle around her, she was ready to accompany him. Gently drawing her arm within his own, they passed out of the room, and stepped on to the Balcony that ran along the entire length of the South of the building and joined the broad Terrace below by means of a flight of marble steps. At the extreme end this Terrace overlooked the rich *partierre* which, although late in the season, still sent forth its delicious perfume, borne upwards on the soft breeze of the evening.

"He has caught at the Indian bait. We have hooked our fish; our next care is to have him safely landed. The poison of love has not, as yet, developed itself. The Scarlet Fever will quench all other maladies, at least until the seas will divide them," and with a self-satisfied smile upon her still pretty features, Mrs. Fraudhurst betook her self to her own apartments to concoct an epistle for the information of Ralph Coleman.

For nearly an hour did the fair young creature and the youth, who had ever been to her as a brother, pace up and down the moonlit Terrace. Arthur related all that passed between himself and her uncle. She was as much delighted as himself at the prospect which had thus suddenly opened before him; the only drawback was that he would be absent so long from Vellenaux.

"But you will write frequently, and come home whenever you can procure leave of absence. And to think that you will not leave us for three months. We will have a merry time this Christmas, Arthur, will we not? and wind up with a fancy ball on the eve of your departure. Oh, it will be delightful," said the excited girl, carried away by the idea of such an event.

Verily, Mrs. Fraudhurst had divined truly. Love's insidious poison had not yet developed itself in the bosom of either. They returned to the drawing room, and, after singing together some of their favourite pieces, they retired for the night.

It was near morning before Carlton fell asleep; even then his brain continued to be disturbed by exciting dreams. Now leading a charge of horses or storming some Indian fortress. Finally he dreamed that he had rescued some Princess or Rajah's daughter from becoming the prey of an enormous Bengal tiger, the head of which, strange to say, bore a striking resemblance to Mrs. Fraudhurst; that the Rajah, in return for his services, gave his daughter to him for a bride; that the marriage took place at the little church at Vellenaux. He thought that as the bride approached the altar in gorgeous attire, and was about to place her hand within his, a seraph-like form glided between them and his hand was lovingly grasped by Edith Effingham, when all suddenly vanished in a thunder storm. He awoke with a start and leaped from the bed, for there was a loud knocking at the door and the voice of the old Butler exclaiming, "Master Arthur, master Arthur, Miss Edith desires me to say that she is going to ride over to the Willows this bright morning and wishes to know if you would like to accompany her; she is now on the lawn."

"Thank you, thank you, Reynolds. My compliments to Miss Effingham, and say I shall be most happy to be her escort on the occasion," and hurriedly dressing, was soon by her side, laughing and chatting merrily as they cantered over the green turf on their way to the Bartons. Yet Arthur could not altogether dispel the feelings that arose within him, produced, doubtless, by the strange dreams that haunted his pillow during the night, or early that morning.

"Is not that Tom Barton?" said Edith, pointing to the figure of a man, dressed in sporting costume, seated on the step of a stile, engaged in lighting a small German pipe, his gun leaning against one of the uprights and some half dozen partridges lying on the grass at his feet. As they rode up, Tom advanced to meet them, raised his hat politely to Edith, and shouted out, "Hallo Arthur, old fellow, how are you. Glad to have you back amongst us; not much fun in tramping through the turnip fields alone, although the birds are by no means scarce this season."

"Thank you, I intend to be amongst them, and together, I think we can do some execution. How are the ladies at the Willows? And is pretty little Cousin Kate as capricious as ever?" And here Carlton gave his friend a poke in the ribs with his riding whip.

Edith laughed heartily at the sallie; for his attachment to the lady in question was no secret to her. Tom parried his friend's enquiries as best as he could, and the trio proceeded at a walk in the best possible good humour.

On reaching the Willows they found Tom's sisters and Kate Cotterell on the gallery. Their approach had been observed by old Mrs. Barton, from the window of the breakfast room. They were received with a shower of welcomes, for both Edith and Arthur were general favourites with all the neighbouring families, and especially so at the Bartons.

Of course, Arthur's appointment and approaching departure for India was communicated; all were pleased to hear of his good fortune, though sorry to lose his society.

"You will, of course, call upon Horace and Pauline when you reach Calcutta," suggested old Mrs. Barton, "I dare say you may not recollect him, but he will remember you, although you were but a curly-headed boy when he was last in England. You must take out some letters from us to them."

Edith had a hurried conversation with Kate Cotterell, Julia and Emily Barton, on some little project of her own. This being finished, she beckoned to

Arthur, who was smoking and arranging some matters with Tom Barton at the other end of the gallery; then mounting their horses they rode slowly back to Vellenaux, in time to breakfast with Sir Jasper, who was, by no means, an early riser.

With shooting, (with Tom Barton and some half dozen other College chums,) visiting his acquaintances, and taking long rides through the beech woods and over the downs with Edith, who was an excellent equestrian, for his companion, the first six weeks of Arthur's return passed pleasantly and rapidly away. He then had to post up to London to get measured for his uniform, and general outfit, to say nothing of the numberless commissions which he had been entrusted to execute by his lady acquaintances, in view of the approaching fancy ball. Being his first visit to the Metropolis, Arthur determined to see and hear all that could be and seen heard during his short stay in that wonderful city.

Jack Frost, with his usual attendant and companion, snow, heralded the approach of old Father Christmas, who filed an appearance at Vellenaux on the morning of the twenty-fifth of December, and right heartily was the old fellow welcomed. His advent had been announced at daybreak, by discharges from an old-fashioned field piece which Bridoon (with the permission of his old commander) had mounted on a wooden carriage to commemorate his Peninsular victories, while the Bell Ringers rang out a merry peal from the belfry of the quaint old church in the little village hard by. Then came troops of merry, laughing children, singing and chanting old Christmas Carols, and were rewarded by the old housekeeper with a piping hot breakfast of mince pies, etc., etc.

After morning service in the church, which was numerously attended, the laborers and many of the poorer tenants of the estate were regaled with roast beef and plum pudding, good old October ale and mighty flagons of that cider for which Devonshire is so justly celebrated. During the evening there was a dance and supper in the servants' hall, to which many of the small farmers with their wives, sons and daughters, had been invited, and a right jovial time they had of it. Dancing, songs, scenes from the magic lantern, hunt the slipper, blind man's buff, kissing under the mistletoe, and many other Christmas gambols were the order of the evening,—and, if one might judge from the bursts of mirth and laughter that prevailed, this was very much to the satisfaction of all present.

The worthy Baronet, attended by Edith and Arthur, visited his work people during the dinner in the great barn, addressing words of welcome and kindness to all, nor did he absent himself from the merry-makings in the servants' hall.

"Attention, form a line there!" shouted old Bridoon, the lodge keeper, who was the Sir Oracle of the hour, and had seated himself in a large arm chair beside the enormous fireplace, wherein the Yule logs burnt brightly, darting out forked flames of blue, yellow, and crimson, and sending forth great showers of sparks up the huge old-fashioned chimney like fire-works on a gala night.

"Make way there for the Brigadier and his handsome aides-de-camp." The sharp eye of the old campaigner had caught sight of the party from the drawing room, which had halted in the door way and was looking on highly amused at the merry groups that were footing it bravely, and with untiring energy through the mazes of Irish jigs, Scotch reels and English country dances. On entering, the mirth ceased for a moment out of respect to Sir Jasper. "Go on, my good friends, we came to witness, not to put a stop to your amusement," said the Baronet, as he took a seat in the chimney corner, supported by Edith and Arthur. The dancing was again resumed in about half an hour, and the party rose to retire. Here Reynolds, the old butler, presented his master with a magnum of his favorite port, which the old gentleman tossed off, wishing them all a merry Christmas. This was the moment for which Bridoon had been waiting; he rose and proposed the health of Sir Jasper, Miss Edith, and Master Arthur, and said, "When lying wounded on the bloody field of Salamanca little did I think that I should live to enjoy so many years of peace and comfort in such snug quarters as is now provided for me by my old commander and benefactor, God bless him," Then addressing Arthur he said, "Master Arthur, it does my old heart good to know that you have entered her Majesty's service. You are a good swordsman, a bold rider ('and the best shot in the country,' put in the head game-keeper), no mean qualifications," continued he, "for a Light Dragoon; and I feel certain you will turn out as fine a soldier as the Colonel, your father,—I drink to his memory and your success." Whereupon the veteran raised a massive tankard of sparkling cider to his lips and took a mighty draught, which laudable example was immediately followed by all the men present. The Baronet and his *protégés* then left the hall.

There was open house to all comers until after the New Year, and in this way Christmas had been kept up in that part of Devonshire from time immemorial.

But the great event of the season to the upper tandem of Vellenaux, and its vicinity was the approaching twelfth-night Ball. Sir Jasper had given *carte blanche* to his niece to do as she pleased on the occasion and she did so accordingly.

# CHAPTER IV.

Great was the excitement and preparation going on among those invited to participate in the coming festivities. Of all the places in the county, Vellenaux was considered the most suitable for the purpose of a Fancy Dress Ball. There had not been anything of the kind within a circuit of fifty miles, for at least as many years. The grand old hall, with its banners and knightly armour of different periods, the magnificent apartments filled with curiously carved antique furniture, ancient mirrors and embroidered tapestries, all of which would harmonize with the costumes of those who would figure about for the *nonce*. Of course the characters to be assumed were to be kept a secret until they appeared in the ball room. Edith entered with enthusiasm into all the arrangements necessary on the occasion, and was materially assisted by the good taste and judgment of Arthur, to whom she turned for counsel when at fault as to the grouping of statuary or position of pictures, and the *toute ensemble* of the *salle-a-manger*.

The spacious old picture gallery with its Gothic windows of stained glass was fitted up as the dancing hall. The statuary armour, banners, and ancient weapons of past generations had been brought from the Hall and placed in different positions along the oak pannelled walls, while large bunches of dark green holly with the bright scarlet berries, peeping out here and there was hung between the antique pictures of brave Knights and fair Dames, ancestors of the Coleman family, that seemed to look down from their massive frames upon the fantastic scenes below. The oaken floor was covered with a cloth, figured to represent a tesselated pavement. At the upper end a dais had been erected, surmounted by an antique chair of state, with several others of the same description, but smaller on each side. The orchestra was in a small gallery that crossed the hall at the lower end, the whole brilliantly illuminated by three massive chandeliers, the adjoining apartments were arranged as refreshment and supper rooms.

The Ball was opened with a triple set of quadrilles. The top set, nearest to the dais or place of honour, was composed as follows: Sir Jasper as the fine old English gentleman in doublet and trunk hose, with Edith, looking very lovely, as the Lady Rowena; their *vis a vis* being Julia Barton, in the character of Mary Stuart, attended by Arthur, dressed as a Light Dragoon of the period. The side couples were, Kate Cotterell, bewitchingly pretty, in the costume of Rebecca the Jewess, assisted by Tom Barton as the famous Robin Hood. Emily Barton represented, with very good effect, Maid Marion, under the escort of young Snaffle of the Lancers, who rode over from the nearest Garrison Town to captivate some stray heart by personating Young Lochinvar. The other two sets, figuring in costumes as handsome as they were varied, were made up of the youth and beauty of the neighbourhood, with the exception of the bottom couple of the last set; here, Mrs. Fraudhurst appeared, gorgeously attired, as Sarah, Duchess of Marlborough, with no other for her partner than Ralph Coleman in the garb of Mephistopheles. At the conclusion of the first Quadrille, the Baronet seated himself in the state chair, with his old friends on either side, for their dancing days like his own was now as a thing of the past, but looking on with inward satisfaction at the gay assembly, until the memories of their own youthful days rose pleasantly before them, the rare old wines of the choicest vintage, from the well-stored cellars of Vellenaux aiding to keep up these associations, as Waltzes, Polkas, Mazourkas, followed in rapid succession. Nor was the supper the least agreeable feature of the entertainment, for country life, and country exercise, equestrian and pedestrian, over the frozen earth, were wonderful auxiliaries to the appetite, and both old and young did ample justice to the good things that were provided for them.

The Duchess and Mephistopheles kept watchful eye on Edith and Arthur, but their joyous light-heartedness, and that, too, on the eve of his departure, convinced the two conspirators that all was going on as satisfactorily as they could desire. After supper, Sir Roger de Coverly, the Triumph, and other old-fashioned country dances were introduced, followed by questions, answers and forfeits, and other Twelfth-night games, which were entered into with such spirit and animation, that showed how thoroughly they were enjoyed by those who participated therein, and it was universally allowed by all present to be the most charming thing of the kind they had ever attended, and the grey dawn of day appeared on the eastern horizon ere the last vehicle drove away from the hospitable mansion of Sir Jasper Coleman.

On the afternoon of the following day, Arthur was to leave Vellenaux for Southampton en route for the East. He had put off his leave takings until the last moment, and he now entered his patron's private library to say farewell. The parting was more like what might have been expected between a kind father and a favourite son. "Remember, Arthur," said the kind old Baronet, in conclusion, "that, should your regiment be suddenly ordered home, it will always afford me the greatest pleasure to receive you here whenever the duties of your position will admit of your visiting us." Here he shook him cordially by the hand, placing as he did so, a draft on a Calcutta house for three thousand rupees.

Hastily ascending the grand staircase, Carlton made his way to the drawing room. His adieu to Mrs. Fraudhurst was courteous and polite, but there was no exhibition of kindly feeling or sympathy evinced by either.

Now, although Arthur and Edith in their long rides together had canvassed over the subject of his departure repeatedly, and the great benefit he was likely to derive therefrom till they had quite accustomed themselves to the idea, yet, when the moment arrived, a deep feeling of regret visibly agitated them both, a feeling which they had never before experienced, and which there was now no time to analyze. The unbidden tear rose to Edith's eye as he clasped her hand within his own, and unable to control himself any longer, he gently drew her towards him and imprinted a loving kiss on her rosy lips. The next instant he was gone. No word of love had ever been spoken between them, and this was the first time that their lips had ever met. At that moment Mrs. Fraudhurst had looked up from her embroidery, but not in their direction; she was too discreet for that, her glance rested on one of the large mirrors at the opposite end of the room, wherein was reflected the full length figures of the two young friends. The salute did not escape her notice, nor did she fail to mark that the deep crimson blush that diffused itself over Edith's beautiful features certainly was not one of displeasure.

"Gone, but not a moment too soon," she muttered half aloud. Then turning to address a few words to Edith found that she also had left the apartment; gone, doubtless, to seek the privacy of her own chamber.

On reaching Calcutta, the young Cornet presented himself at the hospitable Bungalow of the Bartons, and was by them cordially received. The pretty little Mrs. Barton and Arthur had not previously met, he being at College when she had paid her wedding visit to Devonshire, but nevertheless, she was much pleased to have so handsome a cavalier, to occupy a seat in her barouche while driving along the Chowringee road or cantering by her side across the Esplanade or round and round the stand while listening to the delightful music of the band, as was their usual custom of an evening.

Good, easy Horace Barton had got over that sort of thing, for after returning from the Suddur Aydowlett, he would seek the quiet of his sanctum sanctorum, and with his Hooka and iced Sherbet, would regale himself until the dressing bell rang for dinner, after which he would entertain Arthur with stories of the Pindaree War, the suppression of Thuygee, and relate wonderful feats of looting, perpetrated by the most expert robbers in the world, the Bheel tribes.

"But, my friend," said Horace, on one of these occasions, "the greatest drawback to a young soldier's advancement in this country, is the great facility that is afforded him for getting into debt; and should you unfortunately fall into the difficulty, I strongly advise you to draw on your paymaster, go under stoppages or apply to a friend, but not under any circumstances have recourse to those scourges of the country, the native Sheroffs or money-lenders, and in order to fix your attention to this matter, I will relate a circumstance that occurred to a friend of mine some years ago, which will, I think, prove to you the danger of having anything to do with those gentry, as you might not escape their clutches as my friend ingeniously did.

"There was no denying that Harry Esdale was the handsomest, gayest and most popular man in the station, and was generally to be found taking the lead in any thing that promised fun and frolic. In fact, no ball, party, picnic, cricket-match, race or private theatricals were considered complete without him. Having little else to depend upon besides his pay, no wander that his pecuniary affairs became embarrassed and were to him a source of great annoyance and trouble. To extricate himself for the time being from this unpleasant dilemma, he had recourse to the native Sheroffs, from whom he had borrowed from time to time certain sums of different amounts at an enormous rate of interest, until at last he found that he was totally unable to free himself from his difficulties, or evade his creditors, who haunted him night and day, dogged his steps, and presented themselves most inopportunely when they were least expected or desired.

"He had procured a furlough to Europe, which alone would relieve him from his tormentors, but alas, he was too well watched to admit of his leaving the Presidency. Affairs were in this unpleasant state when a circumstance occurred, which he very adroitly took advantage of, in order to elude the vigilance of his native persecutors.

"It so happened that in his troop there was a man that bore a striking resemblance to him in height and figure, as well as in feature. Just at this particular juncture, and when his creditors were most clamorous for settlement, this man died in the Regimental Hospital. On this circumstance coming to his knowledge, it struck him that he might turn it to his own advantage, could he but obtain the co-operation of the Surgeon and one or two of his brother officers. This he soon effected, so great a favourite as he was could not be refused, besides, was it not a glorious thing to outwit those native dealers in extortion?

"The body of the late Trooper was secretly removed from the Hospital to Esdale's Bungalow, dressed in his full uniform and laid on the bed; a pistol was then discharged into the mouth of the corpse, and the head and pillow besmeared with blood, disfiguring the face considerably; the pistol was then placed on the bed, close to the right hand, and there was all the appearance that death had been caused by suicide.

"Fortunately there was a Ball at Government House that evening; this accounted for his being in full dress. His absence was noticed by many, and later in the evening the startling intelligence was announced that Captain Esdale, had destroyed himself by blowing out his brains while laboring under a fit of temporary insanity. This report spread like wildfire throughout the native town and soon reached the ears of his creditors, who flocked to the Bungalow like so many vultures, fighting and scrabbling with each other for admission, in order that they might secure for themselves whatever effects might be in the Bungalow, but were informed by the guard which had been placed there that nothing could be touched until after the funeral, which took place in a few days with all the pomp and ceremony necessary on such occasions.

"All this time Esdale was snugly stowed away in a little room in the Bungalow of one of his brother officers, and in about a fortnight, when the hubbub caused by this event had subsided, and the vigilance of the money lenders withdrawn, they being completely outwitted, he quietly stepped on board the English Mail.

"A few months after reaching England, he obtained some cash from his governor, and through the agency of a friend who offered his creditors an amount equal to what Esdale had received with an interest of seven per cent added. This they had at first rejected, but seeing no hope of any other settlement, at last concluded to accept and delivered up the I.O.U.'s they had against Esdale. Imagine the surprise and vexation of these people some two years after on seeing the identical Harry Esdale, who many believed they had seen buried, coolly smoking his cheroot in the mess verandah, or basking in smiles of the fair ones as they cantered gaily across the midan after the heat of the day had passed." Horace would, doubtless, have added other words of warning and advice, but Arthur was summoned to attend the Madame Sahib, either in her drawing room or in the spacious verandah, where she entertained her friends. And for nearly a month did he enjoy this kind of life, until he began to believe that India was not the infernal hole that it had been represented to him by Snaffle of the Lancers (who, by the way, had never been there); and in his letters to Edith he gave a glowing account of the city of Palaces and the fascinating Mrs. Barton.

But it must not be supposed that these matters dwelt long in Arthur's mind, for a more engrossing subject was ever before him, and that was the profession he was now entering upon, and the probabilities of his attaining a position in the service equal to that held by his father, and he started to join his regiment with a determination to accomplish this desirable end, or perish in the attempt.

The district through which he had to pass in order to reach head quarters was a wild one. There were also several Bheel villages along the route, nor was there any scarcity of wild beasts in that region, but to Arthur this was not at all alarming. He had read of adventures and difficulties that had been met with by officers of the India army while travelling from one station to another, besides he had a strong desire to engage in the exciting sport of tiger hunting, boar spearing, etc., within the Indian jungles.

On quitting Calcutta, his good friends gave him a *carte blanche* to visit them whenever duty or pleasure should bring him into their neighborhood.

Fortunately for him a small party of Sepoys escorting treasure to a station not far distant from the one in which his regiment was quartered, were to start from Calcutta the same morning. This party he was directed to take charge of as far on the road as he was going. Nor was his journey without an adventure as the following incident will show:

Within the deep shadow of a grove of stately tamarind trees that grew on the roadside, and distant about half a mile from a large and populous Bheel village the tent of our young traveller had been pitched.

It was a lovely night, Corinnua in her glory diffused her soft silvery light far and near rendering the shades of the jungle still more deep by contrast. All was hushed in silence; the busy hum in the village had ceased and no sound broke on the silent night, except the occasional bark of the Parrier dog, or the cry of the lurking jackall and the measured tread of the native sentinel, as he paced to and fro in front of the door of the tent. The remainder of the small guard were soundly sleeping in a little routie tent on the opposite side of the road.

Arthur had been out shooting the latter part of the afternoon and evening, and had, as usual, taken from the village several natives as guides and beaters. On his return he had called them to the door of his tent, opened one of his trunks, and out of a bag, containing two or three hundred rupees, paid them liberally for their trouble; one of the party he noticed appeared to eye the bag with a greedy, covetous eye, but he said nothing, and the party left, seeming well satisfied with what they had received. After indulging in a bath he was ready for the evening meal, which consisted of chicken, curry or broiled partridge with several etceteras, which he washed down with a bottle of Allsopps' pale ale, and betook himself to his easy chair and cheeroot under the majestic Tamarinds, which were undulating gently in the soft breeze of the evening.

There was a small shade lamp burning on the camp table by the side of the iron cot, on which Arthur had thrown himself, being somewhat tired of his ramble in the jungle. He had taken up a volume of the Pindaree war, but had not perused more than a dozen pages when he felt drowsy and sleepy. He had accustomed himself to sleep with his revolver under his pillow, his right hand grasping the handle. Somewhere about eleven o'clock he was lying on his back with his left arm thrown across his chest, and his hand over his face, half asleep and half awake, he fancied he heard a sound similar to that made by sand rats or rabbits while burrowing. The sinister look of the Bheel he had paid in the evening instantly flashed across his mind. Separating his fingers, sufficiently to admit of his seeing through them, he glanced in the direction from which the sound proceeded, and waited patiently, keeping a firm grasp of his pistol. Presently the sand beneath the wall of the tent near the foot of his cot gave way gradually, and a small aperture presented itself, which increased by degrees. By and by the head and shoulders of the identical Bheel showed themselves inside the tent; his hawk eye darted a rapid glance all around, but most especially at the prostrate and apparently sleeping form of Carlton he then drew the remainder of his body, which was perfectly naked, through the aperture and stood erect and for a few seconds remained at the foot of Arthur's bed, and listened to the heavy breathing which he effected; then, with a gliding motion, moved towards the trunk containing the rupees, but still keeping his face half turned in the direction of the bed so that he could observe the slightest alteration, should any be made in the position of its occupant, he then endeavored to force open the lid with his creese, but finding he could not succeed in this, he took from behind his ear a small piece of wire, with which he attempted to pick the lock, but in order to effect this he had to rest his eye on the key hole for a second or two. This was the moment for which Arthur had been anxiously waiting. Instantly the eyes of the Bheel were withdrawn from him. He brought his revolver from under his pillow, and passing it beneath the light coverlet, placed the barrel across his left leg, which he gently raised, at the same time removing the cloth clear of the muzzle, brought it in line with the ribs of the robber and fired. The bullet went straight to the heart, and the ruffian Bheel fell dead without uttering a groan or sound.

"What is the matter," enquired the sentry, stopping at the door of the tent, which had been closed to keep out the night dews.

"Nothing," Arthur had promptly replied, "I have discharged my pistol by accident, and am going to reload it, that is all. But when the Nique comes with the relief tell him to send the Havildar to me, I wish to speak to him." The sentinel then resumed his walk up and down his post. Arthur then with his hands quietly enlarged the hole by which the robber had entered, into which he pushed the body and covered it with the sand which had been thrown up, and the tent resumed its original appearance; then, after washing his hands and refilling the empty chamber of his revolver, he dressed himself for the march.

At twelve o'clock the Havildar made his sallam at the tent door. "Come in, Havildar," said Carlton, "I have changed my mind; instead of marching at four a.m., the usual hour, I wish to start with as little delay as possible. Go round, wake up the cart men and have the cattle put to with as little noise as practicable, fall in the guard, and, when we have moved off some distance, I will tell you the reason of this change in the hour of marching. Let everything be done as quietly as may be; also tell the Syce to bring my horse round directly." The Havildar received his orders (native like) without remark, saluted and went to see them carried out. When the escort had got about a mile from where they had encamped, Arthur related what had taken place in his tent the night previous. This was a sufficient inducement for them to accelerate their speed to the utmost in order to get beyond the precincts of the Bheel, as they well knew that in the event of the discovery of the body the whole village would turn out *en masse* to revenge his death, but having some four hours start Arthur and his party arrived at the station—where he was to part from them—without molestation or pursuit, as far as he was aware of.

# CHAPTER V.

This adventure fully developed his coolness and courage when aroused to immediate action by any unexpected danger. This gained for Arthur the favorable opinion of his brother officers. Although he, on joining, made no mention of the circumstance, until in course of casual conversation the affair leaked out. Soon after joining he wrote to Sir Jasper informing him of his safe arrival, and to Edith a long and interesting account of his journey from Calcutta to Karricabad, in which he portrayed with faithful accuracy his encounter with a Bheel, and many other incidents which he thought likely would interest or amuse her. In describing the scenery and general features of the wild districts he had to pass through, he said:

"After traversing for miles the hot and dusty plains of Hindostan, quite unexpectedly you will come upon a tope or grove of fruit trees, planted in regular rows, with a well or tank of spring water, and a place to bathe in built in the centre, where the weary and way-worn traveller could bathe and wash away the heat and dust of the road, and cool his parched throat with a draught of the pure element, gather as much of the rich fruit as he may wish, to appease his appetite if hungry; then, in the soft mossy grass, beneath the overhanging branches which effectually protect him from the heat and glare of the sun, enjoy a sound sleep, awake refreshed and proceed on his way rejoicing. In European countries where hotels and places of accomodation are to be met with at every turn, this may appear of little moment, but in the East where there are no such places to obtain food or shelter from the powerful rays of the sun, this is an inestimable boon. On enquiring how these Topes or groves came to grow in places so far distant from any other cultivation, I was informed that they were planted by rich high caste natives, as a penance that was imposed upon them by the Brahmin priests for sins of omission or commission against their creed. By the way, I heard the other day a good story concerning these said Topes. It appears that a certain ensign of the Company's service, who had been furnished with his commission and outfit by an elderly maiden aunt of a serious and pious turn of mind, whose positive injunctions to him on leaving England were that he was not to attempt to impose upon her with any account of dangers, difficulties, or surprising adventures that were not strictly true, for she hated liars, and would cut him out of her will if she detected him indulging in anything of the sort; but requested that he would write to her a full, true and particular account of his first battle, should he be engaged in one.

"At the commencement of his first campaign he wrote to the old lady a long descriptive letter, but unfortunately he did not pay sufficient attention to his orthography, and so came to grief, for one paragraph of the letter ran thus:

"'Our entire brigade, ten thousand strong, halted about six in the morning, and by seven the whole of the tents were snugly pitched, and we were taking our breakfast comfortably in the tops of trees which grew on both sides of the road.'

"He spelt the word Topes without the capital or letter e. Tents for ten thousand men pitched in the tops of trees. Oh, was there ever such a monstrous falsehood, and the poor old lady fairly shook from head to foot with pious indignation. The letter was returned to the writer without remark or comment, and she was never again heard to mention the name of her nephew, and on her death, which occurred soon after, it was found that she had bequeathed the whole of her property to establish a mission for diffusing the Gospel truth among the natives of the Fiji Islands, and the unfortunate victim to bad spelling was left lamenting."

In another of his epistles to the fair young girl in merry England, he winds up with the following: "Much has been said and written concerning the sagacity of some animals, especially the elephant, horse and dog, but the other day I was an eye witness to a fact which developed the cunning, reason, instinct, or call it what you will, of the Indian Jackall. Having sauntered from my tent in the cool of the evening through some wild cotton plants, down to a clump of shady trees that grew at no great distance from the river, I sat down to enjoy a cigar, and while so doing I observed the following incident: A jackall, one of the largest I believe I had ever seen, came quietly out from the cover of the jungle and made for the river, having in his mouth a large bunch of cotton; curious to know to what purpose he intended applying his mouthful, I watched him. Having reached the water's edge he turned deliberately round and faced in the direction where I was seated, but not in view, then depressing his bushy tail he gradually backed into the water; very slow, indeed, was his backward movement, but on gaining the centre of the somewhat shallow stream his whole body became submerged, leaving nothing visible above the water but the tip of his nose; suddenly he dived, and reappeared on the opposite bank. After giving himself a good shake, he scampered off, apparently in high glee, leaving the cotton floating on the surface of the water. Determined to find out if possible the meaning of this strange proceeding, I walked to the river's bank, and wading some paces in contrived, with my long riding whip, to get hold of the piece of cotton. You may judge of my surprise on finding it to be actually alive with enormous flees. The cunning jackall had taken this effectual means of ridding himself of his troublesome companions."

But ere long scenes of a much more stirring character engaged the attention of our young soldier, and letter-writing had to a considerable extent to give way to the flashing of the sabre and the blurr of the trumpet. The Punjaub was again swarming with a discontented population, whose warlike natures rendered them a most formidable foe for everywhere it was acknowledged that the Seik soldiery as a body were very effective, and their cavalry the finest horsemen in the country. These had yet to be conquered and the bloody fields of Mooltan and Chillianwalla had to be fought and won, and the campaign on the Sutlej brought to a successful termination, ere the troops about to be engaged could return to peaceful quarters.

These brave, but now lawless people, rendered desperate by the internal commotion of petty factions under different leaders, each seeking his own personal aggrandizement, endeavored to throw the onus of the coming struggle on the shoulders of the British Government, though it was patent to all nations, European and Asiatic, that it had been brought about by the Punjaubees themselves.

The bloody fields of Allewal and Sabranon, where they had been severely beaten, was not sufficient to deter these dusky warriors or prevent them from again trying their strength with the paramount power in India, formidable as they knew it to be from past experience, but it is doubtful whether the Seik soldiery ever seriously thought, although they often hauntingly boasted of fighting with the greatest power in Hindostan, until within two or three months of the first battle, and even then the rude and illiterate yeoman considered that they were about to enter upon a war purely defensive, although one in every way congenial to their feelings of pride and national jealousy. To the general impression of the Seiks, in common with other Indian nations, that the English were and are ever ready to extend their power, is to be added the particular bearing of the British Government toward the Punjaub itself.

Throughout this campaign it was by the fortune of war determined that Arthur's Regiment should serve, and among the brave men who rode in its ranks no heart beat higher or bosom burned with greater military ardor at the prospect of glory now opening before them, than that of Arthur Carlton, for with him promotion was the oyster to be eagerly sought for, but which could only be opened by the sword, and no service, however dangerous, must be shirked, in order to attain this desired end.

"Gentlemen, it affords me much pleasure to be able to announce to you that I have just received the order for the Light Dragoons to proceed forthwith and join the field force now advancing towards the river Sutlej, for the purpose of reducing the strong fortress of Mooltan, and capturing its Dewan, the notorious Moolraj, who for some time past has been sowing the seeds of disaffection amongst his subjects, and has at last succeeded in inducing the Seiks and others to take up arms and act offensively against our Government. This, of course, can lead to but one result—their overthrow and ultimate defeat; but it will also give our regiment an opportunity of gaining fresh laurels and again proving to these fellows how dangerous it is to measure weapons with British cavalry. We march the day after to-morrow."

Thus spoke Colonel Leoline, commanding the regiment in which young Carlton was serving as a cornet.

This news, so pleasing to the ear of the soldiers, was received with the utmost enthusiasm by every officer present. They gave three cheers for their gallant leader, and another rouser for the service they belonged to, which made the walls of their mess room ring again, so delighted were they at the prospect of leaving their quiet, humdrum quarters for the dash and excitement of the battle field.

The panorama which opened to the view on the mornings of the—was glorious in the extreme, and one well calculated to awaken feelings of emotion in the most obdurate breast. The dark waters of the Sutlej glittering in the sun's rays as they flowed onward, all unconscious of the bloody strife about to be enacted on its banks: the frowning fortress, with its embattled walls bristling with cannon and swarming with men, whose dusky figures beamed with hate and defiance; around the outskirts of the town were the battalions of Seik soldiery, drawn up under the Dewan Moolraj, watching with savage anxiety the approach of the British force, whose regiments of cavalry that headed the advance opened their glittering ranks to the right and left and made apparent the serried battalions of infantry and the frowning batteries of cannon.

The scene was grandly magnificent. The eye included the whole field and glanced approvingly from the steady order of one foe to the even array of the other. All this spoke gladness of mind and strength of heart; but beneath the elate looks of the advancing warriors there lurked that fierce desire for the death of their fellow-men which must ever impel the valiant soldier.

With the general details during the progress of the siege our story has little to do,—suffice it to say that it was a bloody and protracted affair. The Mooltanees fought with their usual desperate valor, but they had to cope with men who never turned their backs upon a foe when the fiat of battle had gone forth, who scorned to yield even when greatly outnumbered, and regarded defeat, if not actually a crime, an imperishable disgrace; and so the strife waged fast and furious up to the closing hours of the conflict.

The siege and train heavy ordinance of the besieging force hurled their ponderous shot and shell against the masonry and buildings that defended the town and citadel, destroying, crushing, and burning with terrible effect, while the field artillery poured forth continuous discharges of lighter projectiles of every description then in use, sweeping with dreadful result every opposing force that appeared on the walls or other parts of the fortification. Amid the dire confusion and heavy clouds of smoke caused by the incessant cannonading the Infantry effected an entrance among the advanced mounds and trenches of petty outworks, and animated by their partial success, formed themselves simultaneously into wedges and masses, and headed by their brave leaders rushed forward in gallant style. With a shout they leaped the ditch and up swarming mounted the ramparts and stood victorious amid the captured cannon.

The cavalry were effectually employed around and about the outworks of the town, and many a dashing charge and smart encounter took place wherever the enemy's horse made a sortie or sally, which was of frequent occurrence.

Wherever the blows from the tulwa's of the Seik horse rained heaviest there was to be seen the flashing sabre of our young Cornet, cutting and slashing with right good will. The early training of old Bridoon stood him in good stead, and although scarcely twenty-one he had strength and nerve far beyond his age, and on several occasions his conspicuous bravery drew forth the hearty plaudits of his own men and others who witnessed his dashing courage.

In one of the outworks captured from the enemy during the early part of they siege had been erected a field hospital for the wounded, under charge of Assistant Surgeon Dracott of the Light Dragoons. Now it so happened that on the day of the grand attack a party of Seik horse in attempting to effect a retreat from the town were met by the Dragoons, and after a severe contest driven back and pursued as far as it was thought advisable. A number of these fellows turned down a narrow passage in hopes of escaping into the country at another point less guarded, and in so doing came suddenly upon the hospital alluded to, in which there was a considerable number of poor fellows who had been more or less hurt during the attack. Filled with rage and discomfiture at the failure of their first attempt, and seeing the place was guarded only by a small party of Sepoys, for whom they had a supreme contempt—for the independent yeomanry warriors of Afghanistan and the Punjaub held in light estimation the hired native soldiery of Southern India. There were numerous instances on record during the Afghan and Seik wars where the men of the North were seen, sword in hand, to attack the Company's Sepoys, beat down or turn aside their bayonets, and with the other hand drag them from the ranks by their cross belts and slay them. Even when run through the body they have been known to seize a firm grip of the musket until they had dealt a fatal blow to their antagonist and both fall together mortally wounded, so hostile and revengeful were they one to another when engaged in conflict, creed against creed, for the Sepoys of the South were, as a rule, Hindoos, while the Seiks and Afghans were Mahomedans—they conceived the brutal design of destroying the Hospital and ruthlessly putting to death all they could lay their hands on, in revenge for the morning's defeat, then escape to the plains beyond the town. After a few moments' consultation they commenced the onslaught; the Sepoy guard made but a feeble resistance to these powerful horsemen, they threw down their arms and fled in haste leaving the poor invalids to their mercy.

Draycott the moment he guessed their design sprang on to his horse, which fortunately stood ready saddled at the door of the Surgery, and rode straight at the leader of the party, a huge, burly Seik, and engaged him; but he with his light sabre, and less powerful arm, was no match for the Mahomedan soldier, who with one blow smashed the regulation toasting fork, and with his left hand seized the Surgeon by the shoulder, and was forcing him backwards preparatory to giving him the final thrust through the throat; the other scoundrels being engaged in beating down the bayonets of the guard. At this critical moment, and before a man of the wounded had been touched, about a score of troopers, headed by Carlton, appeared on the scene of action, and entirely changed the programme. With a single stroke of his flashing sabre, Arthur dealt their leader such a blow that he was fain to release his hold on Draycott and turn to defend himself; by this time the conflict had become general fierce and bloody.

"Death to the cowardly ruffians; save our wounded comrades," shouted Carlton, as, with a vigorous thrust he sent his weapon deep into the chest of his dusky opponent, placing him at once and forever *hors de combat*. Imitating the dashing conduct of their youthful leader the Dragoons fought as British Soldiers can fight when their mettle is up, and roused by the gallant bravery of their pet officers, in less than twenty minutes from the striking of the first blow every one of the Seik horse were either cut to pieces or taken prisoners. The report of the encounter was spread far and wide, and not a man in the regiment, from the colonel to the trumpeter stood so high in the estimation of both officers and men throughout the Brigade as did our hero. Conspicuous bravery on the battle field seldom fails to elicit rapturous applause from every branch of the service.

The fall of Mooltan and the capture of its Dewan Moolraj did not, as had been anticipated by many, put an end to the campaign. Disaffection and disloyalty had spread throughout the country, and the Seiks were everywhere arming to resist what they were pleased to assert was the intention of the East India Company, namely: the subjugation of the entire country of the five rivers; and large masses of soldiery, under experienced leaders, had congregated on the plains eager for the fray. Not many days elapsed after the reduction of Mooltan before the army received orders and pressed on with all expedition to that part of the country where the battle of Chillianwalla was to decide the question at issue between the contending forces.

The result of the first day's struggle was undoubtedly very much in favor of the Seiks, and can only be accounted for in this way: The followers of the Prophet had for a considerable time been massing themselves under experienced leaders and had established their position in a manner best suited to resist the advancing foe, this they were enabled to do by their thorough knowledge of the the country, without any great exertion or hardship, being undisturbed, and certain that the enemy could not approach but in a certain direction, and that point alone had to be watched. But not so with the British. Long forced marches, outlying pickets, advance guards, and all the harrasing fatigues incident to moving through an enemy's country had to be borne. This to a considerable extent wearied the European soldiery, though it could not dispirit or discourage them, and again they were suddenly attacked ere they were well prepared to do battled. Yet they pressed on to a scene which was to terminate in so bloody a conflict. But the second day told a very different tale; whatever advantage had been gained, during the early stage of the fight, was not only nullified, but their successes became a sort of *Ignis Futuris* that lured them on to their destruction, for during the night the British were reinforced by a column of fresh troops from Bombay and the action opened with twofold vigor, and so the mighty tide of battle rolled on. Towards evening the decisive blow was struck; the Seiks were beaten at all points and fled in wild confusion and dismay, leaving their unconquerable antagonists masters of the field.

"Colonel," said an aide-de-camp, dashing up at full gallop, "your regiment will move one hundred and fifty paces to the right," and then, touching his horse with his spur, darted off in another direction. "Threes right forward," and the Dragoons moved to the position assigned them. A brigade of guns that had been brought up under cover of the cavalry now opened upon the advancing Seik horse with terrible effect, throwing them into such confusion as to prevent them from rapidly reforming. At this moment the order was received for the Dragoons to wheel into line and charge, and ere the Seiks had recovered, were among them, and the flower of the enemy's cavalry had to give way before the impetuous charge of our light Dragoons. There were more hand to hand encounters in this affair than has been recorded in any other engagement of the campaign. During the melee, one of the commanding General's A.D.C.'s had a narrow escape. A powerful looking Seik rode at him, but on coming within arm's length the staff officer's horse stumbled over some dead or wounded men; the sword of the dusky warrior was raised to give the blow, which must have proved fatal, and in another moment there would have been a vacancy on the General's staff, but Arthur, who had been hewing with might and main within a few yards of the spot, seeing the imminent peril of his countryman, dashed up, shortening his sabre as he did so, and, with a powerful thrust, sent it clean through the body of the Seik; the blow intended for the head fell harmless on the plated scales of the epaulet of the aide as he recovered himself in the saddle.

"Thanks, Carlton, my dear fellow, for this good service; I will not forget it, should it ever come to my turn to assist you in any way," was all that could be said in the hurry and excitement of the conflict, for the tide of battle still rolled on. A two gun sheet battery which had been committing great havoc on a column of infantry, was still throwing grape and canister with murderous effect. These discharges had again and again swept through the little party. The Seik gunners stood manfully to their guns until the Infantry came within fifty yards of them. "Charge, men, charge," shouted a very handsome officer of the Bombay Fusiliers, "they cannot stand the bayonets of the old Toughs. Forward." The men sprang to the charge, and about one hundred of the Fusiliers to the very teeth of destruction, facing inevitable death with a coolness and fearlessness so characteristic of the British soldier. But a body of the enemy's horse suddenly appeared on the flank of the column of Infantry compelling them to form square to resist cavalry, and thus the brave little party were placed in a precarious position, being cut off from their supports. A withering volley from the right and rear face of the square, followed by a rapid file-firing from the standing ranks, emptied quite a number of saddles and drove the troopers off.

An officer of Dragoons at the head of a party of his men rode at the Seik artillerest, who, with the exception of two, abandoned their guns and were endeavouring to escape by retreat, but they were all either cut down or captured. The two who yet remained at their post waited for the Infantry to advance sufficiently close to make their fire tell with murderous effect, they then raided their lintstocks to fire, which must have proved horribly fatal to the Fusiliers, when Arthur Carlton, for it was he who led, appeared out of a cloud of dust and smoke close to the Battery. Leveling his pistol, he shot down one of the Seik gunners, the lintstock of the other was within a few inches of the vent. A second more and a frightful gap would have been made in the ranks of the advancing Fusiliers.

A shout that can only be given by a British throat, broke on the ear of the unfortunate artillerest, who hesitated for a moment. It was his last, for a down stroke from Arthur's flashing sabre fell upon his neck, separating the head from the body. The Fusiliers dashed up, and the battery that dealt so much destruction among the Infantry was captured at last.

"Splendidly done, by Jupiter. Those men are the Fusiliers of the Bombay column, are they not? and who is that cavalry officer?"

"Cornet Carlton, Light Dragoons, your Excellency; the same officer who saved your Excellency's despatch and my life, that I mentioned to you some half hour since," was the earnest reply, of one of the aides. "Gallant fellow, bravely done, only a Cornet, must have his Lieutenancy, Hargraves, see that I do not forget this in my despatches to the Government to-morrow." Then, turning to his Chief of Staff, said, "Give orders for the Dragoons and Light Artillery to pursue for half an hour. The enemy is beaten at all points, and get the Infantry under canvass with as little delay as possible." "The action is over," said the Commander-in-chief, closing his field glass, and with his staff left the ground. And thus, after two days hard fighting, the name of Chillianwalla was added to the list of victories that has been emblazoned on the page of history, showing the prowess and valour of British troops in India, and the name of Arthur Carlton was added to the list of Lieutenants borne on the muster roll of the Light Dragoons.

It is not our intention to take the reader over the battle fields of Peshawa, suffice it to say that our Dragoon, with his regiment, scoured the plains of the Punjaub up to the very mouth of the Iron Kybre itself, which had proved fatal to so many of our gallant countrymen.

A group of officers had assembled around the withered and charred stump of a large tree, chatting and smoking, the ruddy glare of the neighboring camp fire throwing its fitful light upon the uniform and accoutrements of the little party, showing them to be no other than our old friends of H.M. Light Dragoons, waiting for the order to commence their morning's march.

"Why are we not on the move?" enquired Major Hackett, as he joined them.

"Something gone wrong with the baggage, I suppose," responded one of the party, "but here comes old Rations, (for it was by this name that the Quartermaster was usually styled by the men of his Regiment) he, perhaps, can tell us something about it."

"Well, Quartermaster, can you explain the cause of the delay. Have you seen the Colonel, or are we to be kept here all day?" and the Major flung away the end of his cigar with an air of annoyance. The good-humored Quartermaster explained, in somewhat of a round-about way, that everything would be all right in a few minutes.

"Out with it, Davison, tell us what is the row. You don't laugh all over your face and half way down your back for nothing, I know," said Arthur, reining up his horse alongside that of the Quartermaster, who, by the way, was a special friend of our young Lieutenant. "Just illuminate and turn on the gas a little, as it were."

"Well, then, gentlemen," resumed that worthy functionary, "it appears that this morning, on the elephants being brought up to carry the mess and Hospital Tents, one of the number was found to be missing, and the Muccadem declared that it was useless to attempt to put anything extra on the others, for that they would not stir a peg if so overloaded. I did not know what to do in this dilemma; the tents could not be left behind, so I sent for Fortescue, who was in charge of the Government cattle, to ask his advice. In a few minutes he came cantering up. I explained matters. The elephant cannot be far off." At this moment a Muccadem came running up to say that the animal was in the jungle, about a quarter of a mile off, but was refractory and would not budge an inch in the direction of the camp.

"Divide his load among the other four," said Fortescue.

"But they will not carry it, sir," replied the native Inspector.

"I know that as well as you can tell me, but do as I order you."

The Inspector salammed and obeyed, but the animals would not move. "Now take off the load from two and give them a couple of tether chains." This was done, the loads removed, and a long chain, used for camp purposes given to each, who caught them up with their trunks and seemed to know exactly what they were expected to do with them. They were then led into the jungle where the other one was said to be.

"You will see some fun presently," said Fortescue, and he was right, for in a very short time the refractory animal was seen coming into camp at the top of his speed, shrieking and crying, closely followed by the other two, who were thrashing him soundly with the chains that had been given to them for that purpose. There is no doubt they gave him to understand that they did not intend to carry his load for him.

I have heard elephant stories before, but it was most ridiculously absurd to see that great mountain of flesh crying like a whipped child, go down on his knees and quietly receive his burden without any attempt to hurt or molest his keeper.

All the baggage was by this time off the ground; the regiment got the order to advance, which they did with right good will, for both officers and men of the Light Dragoons were equally satisfied to find themselves once more approaching their comfortable quarters in Karricabad.

# CHAPTER VI.

Smiling Spring, with her ever-changing episode of sunshine and tears, had twice come and gone. The gorgeous fields of golden grain had for a second time bent their heads beneath the harvest side, and the autumnal tints of every hue and shade had again fallen on the rich foliage of the magnificent old woods of Devon, while the whirr of the pheasant in the preserves, and the popping at the partridges among the turnips, indicated that the shooting season had once more commenced over the broad lands around Vellenaux.

Things wore much the same aspect as they had done on Arthur's return from College and prior to his departure for the sunny plains of Hindostan some eighteen months since. Sir Jasper was apparently hale and hearty. Edith had finished her education, on which her uncle had spared no expense, for masters and professors had been procured from London to superintend her studies. She was perfectly happy, occasionally receiving letters from Arthur, which always afforded her much pleasure to peruse and think over, and frequently would she detect herself gazing upon his photograph in the pretty little locket he had sent her from Oxford by Tom Barton, and which, since his departure, she constantly wore.

Ralph Coleman's visits had become more frequent of late; this at first did not attract Edith's notice. She had never been prepossessed in his favour, but as her uncle's kinsman, and being heir to the Baronetcy, her deportment to him had ever been polite and affable, but subsequently his attentions became so marked that they aroused her to a sense of his real meaning. Yet she could scarcely bring herself to believe that such was really the case, and but for the delicate hints and inuendos that occasionally fell from the double dealing widow, she would, there is no doubt, have remained for a much longer time unconvinced of his intentions towards her. However, time was passing on and Ralph made up his mind to bring matters to the point. One lovely afternoon, as he was entering the conservatory, he espied the fluttering of a woman's dress among the shrubs and flowers, and on coming nearer, though still at some little distance, perceived a lady walking slowly and as if in deep thought. Feeling quite certain that it was no other than the one he was in quest of, and thanking the fates for giving him the long wished for opportunity, he advanced more quickly and was soon beside Edith (for she it proved to be) before she was aware that any one was near. Turning, with something of a surprised look on her lovely face, she exclaimed, "Oh, how you startled me. I thought you were on the way to London. I am quite amazed to find you here."

"I hope my presence is not distasteful to you," he said, gently, at the same time lifting his hat and bowing low before her. He really cared nothing for the beautiful girl at his side, for he was thoroughly selfish; nor did he care by what means or how low he had to stoop to gain possession of the object wished for.

Edith, knowing her own feelings, and not wishing to say aught to hurt or offend him more than was actually necessary, scarcely knew how to answer him, disliking him as she did. Still she had nothing to complain of, for he had ever paid her the most marked respect. Before she could frame her answer he spoke again, "Edith, I have for some time been wishing to speak to you on a subject very near my heart. I love you dearly and have long done so, will you be my wife, or, at least, give me some hope that my suit may be acceptable at some future time? only give me one encouraging smile, one ray of hope, and I will drudge on patiently until you bid me come to you."

"Oh no," Edith replied, "you must not wait, you must not hope, I can never be yours. Go, leave me." Before she had well finished, Ralph Coleman had seized her little white hands in his strong grasp, and said in a deep, hoarse voice, "Edith, I ask you again will you be mine?"

Surprise, astonishment, and a feeling very like indignation took possession of Edith.

"Mr. Ralph Coleman," she said, "before I answer any more questions, release my hands." As he did so she raised her head proudly, and turning towards him with a heightened color, said, "I have already told you that I cannot love you, and am surprised that it is not sufficient. I thank you for the honor you intended, but beg that you will never mention this subject to me again."

As these words fell upon his ear, Ralph Coleman's face changed and darkened visibly, an evil light came into his eyes, and an ugly frown contracted his brow, then, with a smile, whose meaning could not be mistaken, he said:

"Take care, proud girl, I have sworn that you shall be mine, and by the Heavens above us, I intend to keep my vow, and neither man nor devil shall turn me from my purpose!"

Edith's eyes flashed, her beautiful lips curled in scorn, and her whole face beamed with intense disgust, and with a voice low and deep she said,

"Have a care, sir, beware how you threaten the niece of Sir Jasper Coleman. Before to-morrow my uncle shall be made acquainted with what has just passed, and the character of the man who has partaken so often of his hospitality, and been ever treated with kind attention, he has yet to learn how these courtesies have been returned," and sweeping past him with a look of supreme contempt, Edith was about to pass on.

It was evident that he had gone too far and that she was not a girl to be intimidated by anything that he might say, and at once changed his tactics—

for he was an excellent actor—"Pardon me, Miss Effingham, I know not what I am saying, I am mad. Yes, lady, mad! for your beauty like the moon, makes all men mad, who comes within the sphere of its attraction. Forgive me for thus offending you." Edith turned towards him, and with calm dignity replied, "Promise me never again to revert to this subject, and in no way further molest me, and what has just passed shall be forgiven." He gave the required promise. Edith then pursued her way to the end of the conservatory, passed through the doorway, and on to the terrace where she was met by her Uncle. He observed her heightened color, but as she made no complaint he allowed it to pass without comment.

Ralph Coleman stood for a few moments irresolute. She must, he thought, either be aware that her uncle has left her sole heiress, or else is in love with another, Carlton perhaps. Fool that I was to run so great a risk, and that, at the instigation of that scheming woman. Should she say aught to her uncle on this matter, it would ruin me with him. I will at once seek an interview and endeavour to wheedle him out of a promise to make a codicil in my favor.

Failing in the attempt to secure the hand of the beautiful Miss Effingham, and not daring to risk another trial, as it might spoil the plans he had been contemplating since Edith's dismissal of him, he had kept shy of that young lady during the remainder of his stay, and prior to his departure for London, he had contrived to have a long interview with the Baronet, during which he very ably showed the position that he would hold should the Baronetcy eventually descend to him who was totally unable to support the dignity of the rank that would thus be thrust upon him. So well and ably did he argue this point, that ere he left Vellenaux he extorted a sort of promise from Sir Jasper that he would think the matter over and make a bequest in his favor.

He returned to his office, in deed court, annoyed and disheartened to a considerable extent by the failure of his designs as far as related to Miss Effingham, but his wounded vanity he could afford to bear and hide within his own breast, as he now confidently believed that Sir Jasper would adopt the suggestions he had made to him, and settle, at least, two or three thousand per annum on the successor to the Baronetcy during the said successor's life; and in this frame of mind the Lawyer determined to de vote himself entirely to his profession, and to avoid the pretty Edith, Mrs. Fraudhurst, and Vellenaux, until the present owner should have been gathered to his fathers.

There is perhaps no season of the year in the South of England so pleasing to the eye or more genial to the corporeal faculties than that of early autumn, especially that part of Devonshire which we have selected for the opening and closing scene of our story. Vellenaux, with its varied and picturesque styles of architecture, embosomed, as it were, in rich woodlands, with a perfect amphitheatre of hills on three sides, and ever and anon the soft breezes of the ocean sweeping over the downs, and through the beech woods on the other. It was, indeed, a domain of which any one might have been proud.

It was a lovely evening, the sun had just commenced to dip behind the crest of the adjacent hills, and was sending its golden rays through the bright foliage of the trees and down the long paths that led to the woods hard by. Edith had strolled, book in hand, to her favourite knoll, beneath a stately elm, and was engaged in reading. Her two favourite dogs, fine specimens of the Italian greyhound, chased each other in circles which gradually grew smaller until it brought them to the very feet of their mistress. One placed his small smooth nose in the little white hand that was thrown carelessly on the moss grown roots beside her, while the other, to attract her attention, placed his paw on the page she was reading and looked up in her face. Suddenly their ears elongated and away they bounded, as the noise of horses hoofs were heard approaching in her direction, aroused her from her recumbent position, as Julia Barton, on her quiet little pony, trotted up. She was off in an instant, and running up to her friend, greeted her in the animated, lively way, as was her custom when she had anything to communicate that she thought would please or interest her. "At your studies," she said, taking up the volume that Edith had let fall on her appearance. "Long engagements, a tale of the Affghan war. Oh, oh, thinking of our old playfellow are we?" and the merry girl laughed heartily, "we shall soon hear more of him, for my sister-in-law, Pauline, has just most unexpectedly arrived, and I wish you to know her. She is very charming and improves wonderfully on acquaintance, is very good-natured, and tells such funny stories about the people she lived among, and has a great deal to say about Arthur Carlton. You will come to the Willows to-morrow, will you not, and call on her?" Edith gave the required assent, and Julia, mounting her pony, cantered down the avenue to the lodge gate, where she was joined by a tall, gentlemanly looking man, mounted on a small bay mare, and the two walked their horses at an easy pace down the green lane in the direction of the Willows, and Edith returned to the house in time to dress for dinner, well pleased with the prospect of hearing something of him who was scarcely absent from her thoughts for any great length of time. She did not attempt to analyze her feelings on the subject. It was pleasant to think of her absent friend, and that was sufficient for the present.

Mr. Barton, Sen., or old Mr. Barton as he was usually styled, for he was upwards of eighty years of age, and had been born in the house he now occupied, a good comfortable and substantial, but old fashioned dwelling, which had passed from father to son for several generations. His father had been what is termed a gentleman farmer, and attended personally to the superintending of his acres. His son, the present occupant, had followed his example. He married early in life, but the lady of his choice died young, leaving one son to remind the sorrowing widower of his loss. This was Horace Barton, whom we have already introduced; he chose a different field for his labors, and managed to secure, while yet young, on appointment in India. Our friend Tom and his two sisters, Julia and Emily, were the result of a second marriage, and although there was every comfort to be had, and a good home for all during the life of the old couple, yet it was absolutely necessary that Tom should make his own road through life, and that the girls should, by early marriage, secure for themselves suitable establishments, as the Willows would fall to Horace on the death of his father, and it would not be many years before his term of service in the East would expire, and he would then, doubtless, return to England and occupy the old house in Devonshire.

The arrival of Mrs. Horace Barton from Calcutta had been quite unexpected at the Willows, as no preparatory letter had announced her intentions or arrival in England. Nevertheless she found all delighted to receive her. She had spent the most of her visit to Europe in the gay capitals of Paris and London, and a couple of months was all the time she could spare to remain in Devonshire.

On her first visit she had not been introduced to Miss Effingham, and had only caught a casual glance at her while crossing the lawn, as Edith was returning from a visit to Julia Barton; but on this occasion was determined to become acquainted with her, and find out if she really deserved the high encomiums that had been bestowed upon her by Arthur Carlton. She had anticipated seeing a pretty lively English country girl, but was totally unprepared for the brilliant beauty and perfectly self-possessed manners of Edith, and she always found an attentive listener in her to all she had to relate on the subject of India and Arthur Carlton whenever they met, which was now frequent, for an introduction had taken place between them very shortly after her arrival, and they consequently became on the most intimate and friendly footing. The magnificence of the ancestral dwelling of the Colemans, with its Parks, Parterres and grounds, was quite a novelty to Pauline Barton, and with Edith she traversed the long corridors, picture galleries, and armories with wonderment, for they contrasted strangely with the Pagodas, Temples, and Bungalows in the country where the greater part of her life had been spent (for she had been born there), and she thought that Edith's life must be one of never-ending delight, and for a time it was so, but a sad change was about to come over the bright spirit of her dream of happiness for a time, and perhaps for ever, and dash the cup of joyous light-heartedness from her grasp.

The event so much desired by the man of law took place at a much earlier date than had been anticipated by that gentleman, or, indeed, by any one of his acquaintances as the sequel will show.

"Reynolds," said the Baronet, one evening after dinner, some few weeks after his interview with his worthy cousin, the heir to the title, "place candles in my study, and you need not wait up for me. It is likely that I shall sit writing to a late hour." The old servant bowed, and retired to do the bidding of his master.

After affectionately wishing his niece good-night, and a passing remark to Mrs. Fraudhurst, Sir Jasper entered his study, closing the door quietly behind him.

For a considerable time he paced the room, with his hands crossed behind his back, as was his custom when in a meditative mood. Finally, seating himself at his escritoire, he placed the massive silver candlesticks, with their wax lights, in such a position that the glow would not effect his sight, and arranged his materials for writing to suit him. For a few moments he leaned back in his chair, then selecting a small key from a bunch he always carried, unlocked the centre drawer which contained only a few memorandums and drew it completely out. He next touched a small spring at the side, when a panel of the back slid open, disclosing an aperture from which he took the packet he had brought from London the evening previous to the opening of our story. This was the will and testament of Sir Jasper Coleman, in which he had left his niece, Edith Effingham, sole heiress of all he possessed, with the exception of a gratuity of five thousand pounds to be paid to his *protégé*, Arthur Carlton, within six months after his (the Baronet's) decease, and to be free from all legacy or other duties. Having re-read the document, he laid it on the table beside him and then commenced writing.

Sir Jasper had thus acted without the knowledge of his lawyer, the man with whom he had consulted on every other matter since his succession to the Baronetcy, consequently that gentleman was in ignorance of any such will being in existence. It had been drawn by a competent lawyer residing in one of the suburbs of London, and had been properly witnessed, and was, in every particular, a regular, complete document. The parties present on the occasion knew nothing of Sir Jasper, had never heard of Vellenaux or its owner, and in all probability would never hear of him again, as there was no likelihood of the will being contested. Why he had acted in this manner is hard to say.

The Baronet had finished his letter, and was again musing, and muttering to himself, "Ralph Coleman, you are an unprincipled man. Do you think your attempt to coerce my darling niece to listen to your suit has escaped me. You have failed in that quarter and now come to me to assist you. Well, well as she is safe I can afford to forgive you, and let you have a couple of thousand a year, to enable you to support yourself like a gentleman when the title descends to you." Here the Baronet resumed his pen and commenced the writing of a codicil in behalf of his cousin, Ralph Coleman.

Perfect tranquility reigned throughout the house, all, with the exception of Sir Jasper, had retired to rest, and there was no sound, save the ticking of the old-fashioned time-piece, with its monotonous and never varying tick, tick, and the scratching noise made by the quill as it traced its inky characters on the yet incomplete codicil the Baronet was preparing. The candles had burned low in their sockets, and the fire on the hearth had died out unheeded by him who sat writing line after line. Suddenly a spasm seized him. He, with great difficulty, raised himself from the stooping position over the escritoire, but as he did so, another spasm, more violent than the first, attacked him. He tried to call for assistance, but his tongue clove to his mouth. He was suffocating. He stretched his arm towards the silver bell, which stood on the table, but it was beyond his reach. His head sank on the cushion of the chair. His eyes closed, another convulsive start, and all was over. Sir Jasper Coleman was no more.

For many months past it was customary whenever it was known that Sir Jasper would sit up late, for Mrs. Fraudhurst, on passing the door of his chamber before descending to the breakfast room, to tap and enquire whether the Baronet would come down to his breakfast or have it sent up to him. On the following morning the widow on stopping at the chamber door discovered that it was ajar, and on pushing it gently open found the room was vacant, the bed undisturbed and, it was quite evident from its general appearance, that Sir Jasper could not have passed the night—or any part of it—there. Though startled a little at first, Mrs. Fraudhurst was not long in coming to a conclusion as to what really had happened during the night. It had more than once occurred to her active mind that such might be the manner in which the Baronet's life would terminate. "And the hour I so feared may have come at last," thought she, as the consequences that might accrue to herself, should such turn out to be the case, rose up before her; but she was equal to the emergency; quickly and noiselessly she descended to the private library and, without rapping, entered, closing the door quietly after her.

The morning sun streamed through the stained glass windows, casting their brilliant hues full on the face of the corpse, rendering the pale features more ghastly to look on than the convulsions had left them. Mrs. Fraudhurst was a woman of strong mind, but no feeling, and the presence of death had no terrors for her. She had entered, prepared in her own mind for the spectacle that now presented itself. Her plans had been already arranged, but she had hardly counted on their being so easily executed. With a firm hand she took up the will and unfinished codicil, folded them, and placed them carefully in the bosom of her dress. She now took up the bunch of keys, and replacing the centre drawer, locked it and dropped the bunch of keys into one of the pockets of Sir Jasper's dressing gown, and finding that the open letter related to general business connected with the estate and some charitable institution, left them as she found them, and without one look of pity or regret on her now flushed face towards him to whose liberality she had for years been indebted for a home, with all the comforts and conveniences of life, left the apartment and regained her own chamber without meeting or being seen by any one. Her first act was to securely lock up the papers so feloniously obtained, then, applying cold water to her heated brow, to wait for the ringing of the second bell for breakfast. She could hear the voice of Edith, as her laugh rang out upon the lawn beneath her open window, at the gambols of the two greyhounds.

"Reynolds, ascertain whether Sir Jasper will have his breakfast sent up to him," said Mrs. Fraudhurst, as she and, Edith took their seats at the table, some twenty minutes later.

Edith did not speak, but waited patiently to know if her uncle would come down. There had been a growing coolness between her and the lady who headed the table. She could not but think that there was some complicity between her and Ralph Coleman with respect to herself. She could not tell why this should be, but could not divest herself of the idea, nevertheless.

"My master is not in his own room, and has not slept in his bed," hurriedly exclaimed Reynolds, re-entering the breakfast room. Edith started up, visibly agitated, but not so with the widow, she coolly said, "you had better look in at the library, he was writing there late last night and may probably have thrown himself on the lounge, and fallen asleep there."

"I will go with you," Edith said to the old servant, as she proceeded a little in advance of him.

Mrs. Fraudhurst sat staring blankly out of the window waiting for the result, which she knew must ensue. A loud shriek from Edith rang through the house, and breathless with excitement, Reynolds entered and announced Sir Jasper's death and that Miss Effingham had fainted.

The time for action had now arrived. "He may be only in a fit," said Mrs. Fraudhurst. "I will myself drive over for Dr. Martin. Call Miss Effingham's maid and let her be carried to her own room and properly attended to. I will return with all speed; in the meantime, Reynolds, be sure that no one enters the room. You had better lock the door and take possession of the key as soon as Miss Edith has been removed." After quickly dressing, she proceeded towards the stables to hurry forward the harnessing of the pony phaeton, which was at all times at her disposal, and drove rapidly to the house of Dr. Martin, though she well knew his services would be of no avail, but it was a part of the plan she had matured, and was now carrying out.

Fortunately for her the Rector and Sir Jasper's lawyer and general business agent were at the time with the Doctor in his surgery, consulting on some Parish business and without a moment's delay they proceeded to Vellenaux, the Rector riding with Mrs. Fraudhurst, whose appearance and conduct were well suited to the occasion.

Life was pronounced extinct, and the cause of death was supposed to be a sudden attack of his old complaint, disease of the heart. The lawyer, in the presence of all, placed seals on the escritoire and doors of the study immediately after the body had been transferred to the bedchamber, and wrote to Ralph Coleman, as the only male relation of the late Baronet, acquainting him with what had occurred, and it was not long before that gentleman presented himself at Vellenaux.

# CHAPTER VII.

The morning prior to the funeral it pleased Mrs. Fraudhurst, on meeting Ralph Coleman in the long corridor, to request that worthy individual to grant her a private interview in the general library at eleven o'clock, precisely, the lawyer bowed in the affirmative and passed on.

At the time appointed the widow, in very deep but fashionable mourning, entered the library by one door, and a few minutes later the new baronet presented himself at another. After closing it he advanced to the centre table and waited for the lady to announce the nature of her business with him.

In a low, clear and cold, but perfectly steady voice she thus addressed him, "Some two years since I informed you by letter of the existence of a will in which the late baronet, after paying a gratuity of five thousand pounds to Arthur Carlton, left Miss Effingham sole heiress. In that will the name of Ralph Coleman does not appear. If this document be read to-morrow," she continued after a slight pause, "Vellenaux is lost to you forever."

"But, my dear madam," he replied, "among the late baronet's papers will, doubtless, be found a codicil in my behalf, in fact my cousin distinctly promised me that he would make a suitable provision for the successor to the title."

"And so he would have done had he lived long enough to complete it," was the lady's quiet reply.

"You do not mean to say that you are certain Sir Jasper made no such provision," enquired the lawyer in a quick and excited tone.

"No document of that kind had been executed prior to the baronet's death," she boldly asserted, advancing towards him. "Now listen to me: providing the will in question be not forthcoming after the funeral, the law will declare you heir to the estate. Now, if you swear to me by all that you hold most sacred, that you will allow me one thousand per annum and a suite of apartments at Vellenaux so long as I shall live, no will shall appear, and within one hour after the body of the late Sir Jasper has been consigned to the tomb, you shall become Sir Ralph Coleman and master of Vellenaux and its broad lands."

"But," was the cautious reply of the wily lawyer, "how know I that any will has been made or that the Baronet has not kept faith with me. Your word is all that I have to depend on for the truth or falsity of the statement." He knew her to be an unscrupulous woman, but shrewd withal, and could not bring himself to believe that she would compromise herself so far as to have fraudulently possessed herself of, Sir Jasper's papers, yet her language indicated very strongly that something of the kind was the case.

"If she really has them," he thought, "one thousand per annum would not be too large a sum to purchase her silence concerning them; and as the bargain would be a verbal one, and unknown to any but ourselves, she could not hereafter, by any disclosures that she might make, convict me as an accomplice to the transaction." These thoughts flashed through his mind ere she again spoke.

"Your words, sir, though not complimentary to me, I can excuse, on account of the peculiarity of your present position and frame of mind, and you shall be satisfied of the truth of that which you pretend to doubt," and drawing from her pocket two papers, Mrs. Fraudhurst held them with a firm grasp before him, but in such a position that it enabled him to read every line. "There," she continued, in a low tone, "is the will in question, and the codicil which you so much depend on; are you satisfied?" Then, refolding the papers somewhat hastily, replaced them in her dress and turned to leave the room, remarking as she did so, "I shall return in a few moments, and you must make up your mind as to how you intend to act before I do so."

Ralph had read every line and word, and saw how hopeless was his case unless he closed with the widow's offer, but he would make one more trial to obtain the best position, and as she re-entered said, "Place those documents in my possession and I will swear to fulfil the terms you propose."

"Not so," she replied with a contemptuous curl on her lip, "they remain with me, and I remain here; there will be no difficulty in that. Of course Miss Effingham must find shelter beneath your roof for some time at least, and as you are a single man, you will require some one to superintend your establishment until the future Lady Coleman shall appear on the scene, and ere that event takes place, other arrangements can be made. Accept my conditions and you become one of the wealthiest men in the county. Reject them, and I immediately place both documents in the hands of the late Baronet's lawyer, who is now in the house. I have merely to say that I gathered them from the floor of the study, on the morning of Sir Jasper's death, and that, in the hurry and excitement of the moment, carried them to my own room, unconscious of their importance, until this morning. This statement, true or otherwise, will suffice to account for their being in my possession"

Ralph Coleman would have still hesitated, but her's being the stronger will of the two, he succumbed, took the required oath, and the compact between them was complete. No sooner was this effected than both parties left the place of meeting in the same order as they entered.

Having carried her point and thus secured for herself a comfortable income, together with a handsome suite of apartments within the walls of Vellenaux, which she very naturally concluded would be a permanent home, at least during the life of Sir Ralph, he being completely in her power, as she could at any time, by the production of the late Baronet's will, drive him ignominiously from his present luxurious abode. It is true, in effecting this she would have to seek refuge in a foreign land, yet a vindictive spirit will often, as the old adage runs, cut off the nose to be revenged on the face.

Having gained the mastery of the position, she turned her thoughts in the direction of the new Baronet with a view of inducing him to submit to the matrimonial yoke and by that means establish herself as Vellenaux's envied mistress with the prefix of Lady before her name. However, she could afford to bide her time, feeling certain that in the long run Sir Ralph would yield, her stronger will working on his fears.

The funeral was over. The family vault of the Coleman's in the quaint old church, a little beyond the Park limits, had received the mortal remains of the worthy man, who for forty years had attended divine service within that sacred edifice where the last sad rite for the departed had just been performed. It had been a solemn and imposing ceremony. The cortege passed slowly and silently down the broad avenue of venerable elms, through the Park gate and up the road leading to the old church yard. The superbly mounted coffin, borne on its funeral hearse, whose black plumes, undulated in the soft winds that sighed through the trees, was drawn by six velvet palled horses, and accompanied by mutes, pall bearers and others in all the solemn paraphernalia of woe, followed by the mourning coaches, and the long line of private carriages, some occupied and others empty, for by one of the conventionalities of English well-bred society, one can be present on such occasions by proxy. Your carriage will suffice, should you not feel equal to the task of attending in person. The full, deep, rich tones of the organ poured forth the funeral dirge, as the coffin was carried up the centre aisle and placed on trussels in front of the altar. The pews, gallery and aisles were filled by rich and poor; so much had the late Baronet been respected by friend and tenant. The venerable Rector who performed the service, although accustomed to such scenes, was deeply affected. He had been on the most intimate terms with Sir Jasper, and had never solicited his kind offices on behalf of the poor in vain. Besides, he was more advanced in years than the friend whom he had now consigned to the cold embraces of the grave, for were not his own days numbered and must soon draw to a close?

As the different parties separated on the conclusion of the ceremony, various were the comments and conjectures as to the manner in which Sir Jasper had divided his property, and it was almost universally believed that Miss Edith would come in for a greater part of his wealth and the estate of Vellenaux would undoubtedly become hers.

Sir Ralph, as he must now be called, and others interested in such proceedings, returned, to Vellenaux to examine and hear read the will and such other documents relating to the distribution of the property real and personal of the late Baronet, and great was the surprise of all present except one, when it was announced that, after the strictest search, no will or other document of the kind had been found among the papers of the late Baronet. Mr. Russell, a man of integrity, and well known for the uprightness of his dealings, and who had for upwards of thirty years transacted all the legal business and had the management of the estate of the late Sir Jasper, declared that, to the best of his knowledge no will had been made. This was followed by a statement from Sir Ralph to the effect that it was but a few weeks since, that his cousin, the late Sir Jasper Coleman, had declared to him his intention of making a will in his (Sir Ralph's) favor. Miss Effingham, on being asked, had sent word that she had never heard her uncle say anything on the subject, and Mrs. Fraudhurst, on being interrogated, announced that she had always been of the opinion that Miss Effingham was to be sole heiress of her uncle's wealth, but had never heard Sir Jasper speak of having actually made any will at all. Consequently the law gave to Sir Ralph Coleman the entire property of the late Baronet, whose much-loved niece was thus left a penniless orphan.

Old Reynolds, who had been in the library when it was announced the Baronet had left no will, and that the entire property fell to his cousin, Sir Ralph, immediately summoned the domestics in the servants' hall and related to his astonished hearers what he had heard. Consternation was depicted on the countenance of all, and a wordy colloquy ensued as to what would become of their dear young mistress, and whether they would be discharged to make room for others whom the new Baronet might choose to appoint. The grey-headed old Butler had been at Vellenaux since he was a lad of fourteen, and had known Colonel Effingham, who had frequently, prior to leaving the service, visited his old companion-in-arms, Sir Jasper Coleman, at his favorite residence, felt much concerned that the niece of his old master should have been left unprovided for. "Of course," Said Annette, Edith's own maid "I shall have to return home, for I do not suppose Miss Effingham will remain here very long, as Sir Ralph is a bachelor, and I know for certain that she dislikes him exceedingly."

"But what will madam, the widow, do," enquired the footman.

"Set her cap at him as she did at our poor, dear old master," responded the housekeeper, "No fear, she will take care not to be a loser by the change." "She will, no doubt," suggested another, "keep house for Sir Ralph until he brings home a Lady Coleman, or is persuaded into marrying the widow herself."

It was quite evident, that sympathy ran high in Edith's favour, and that they cared not a jot for the ex-governess or the new master. But they were too well trained to betray what they thought concerning the two last named persons.

The matter was duly talked over throughout the neighbourhood. Some shook their heads but said nothing, and others said a great deal that meant nothing. The Bartons sent a very kind and sympathizing letter to Edith in which they offered her an asylum at the Willows, should she think a little change of scene would in any way reconcile her to the loss she had sustained, they having heard that Miss Effingham had in her grief declined for the present to receive her most intimate friends and acquaintances.

For many days after the funeral Edith kept within the seclusion of her own chamber, alas, hers now no longer, but the property of another and of one whose presence was repugnant to her. With returning consciousness also came the realization of the sad spectacle that had met her view in the private library. She had loved and respected her uncle, and had ever looked up to him as a father, which he had indeed been since the death of her parents, whom she did not recollect, and grief for his loss had outweighed all other thoughts and considerations for the future, and for the first week she gave herself up to inconsolable sorrow. But at length that practical good sense with which nature had endowed her, came to her relief. She stifled the rising sobs in her young bosom and prepared to face the stern realities of life, which must ere long, she knew, force themselves upon her.

To remain in the house of the man she so despised and whose proffered vows of love she had so indignantly rejected, was impossible.

Of the malady which was the cause of her uncle's sudden death, she knew nothing. He had never hinted of its existence, therefore she was totally unprepared and inexpressibly shocked at the suddenness with which he had been struck down, and it was some time before she could sufficiently subdue her agitated feelings to enable her to give any instructions to the household, who, like herself, had been almost stupefied by the calamity.

But not so with Mrs. Fraudhurst; that cold, unfeeling woman cared only for the safety of her own position, and had already arranged what she should do. At her suggestion, no changes were made in the establishment. Every servant was retained, and the business of the estate still left in the hands of Mr. Russell, the former agent, and matters soon resumed their usual routine, as though the late proprietor was merely absent on a visit.

Notwithstanding the precautions taken in order to prevent suspicion from gaining ground that there had been any complicity between Sir Ralph and the widow, which might account for the absence of any legal document making a suitable provision for that niece to whom Sir Jasper was so sincerely attached, there were many who could not divest themselves of the idea that there had been foul play practiced in some way, but as there was nothing tangible to go upon they were compelled to confine their suspicions within their own breasts, and show their sympathy for Miss Effingham by letters of condolence and offers of friendship and protection should she need them; for of course, it was understood by all that her position was materially altered by the apparent fact that Sir Jasper had died intestate.

Both Mrs. Fraudhurst and Sir Ralph were struck with the visible inroad that grief had made in the pale but still beautiful features of Edith, as she entered the drawing room for the first time since her uncle's funeral.

The new Baronet rose as if to conduct her to a seat, but there was something in her eye and manner that checked him, and he contented himself with bowing to her somewhat stiffly, and resumed his chair. She advanced toward the table at which he was seated, with a coolness and self-possession so natural to her, whenever placed in any awkward and trying position; her elegant figure fully developed by the tight fitting habit she wore, and the ringlets of her rich brown hair falling upon her magnificent shoulders from beneath her black riding hat, and in a voice calm, clear and distinct, but without the least bitterness or anger, thus addressed him: "Sir Ralph Coleman, the law, I am told, pronounces you master of Vellenaux and its broad acres. The death of my uncle has left me without a home, but, I trust, not without friends. Do not interrupt me, sir," said she, seeing that he was about to speak, "Your importunities and ungenerous conduct previous to the death of my late lamented uncle and more than father, would, in itself, be a sufficient inducement for me to take the step I am now about to do. It is my intention to leave Vellenaux this morning for the Willows, and request that my personal effects and such property as may have been presented to me by my late uncle may be sent to me there." Then, with a slight inclination of the head towards him, and without a word or glance in the direction of Mrs. Fraudhurst, who was seated at the open window, examining the contents of the post bag, turned and left the apartment. Her intended departure had been made known to the whole of the household by Annette, and, much to her surprise, she found all the servants assembled in the hall to pay their respects to her as she quitted the only home she had ever known. Edith felt deeply their respectful sympathy and parted from them with unfeigned regret. Poor old Bridoon at the Lodge felt keenly for his young mistress, and could not refrain from expressing to her, as she wished him farewell, that there was something wrong about the absence of any will or other document. He would not believe that his dear old master would put off making a provision for his niece until it was too late, and he sincerely hoped that he might live to see the day of her return to Vellenaux as its mistress. This feeling was shared alike by tenantry and servants, for they all had, in some way, been indebted to her for acts of kindness.

"You have been too precipitate, and frightened the bird away," remarked Mrs. Fraudhurst. "But," continued she, after a moment's pause, "perhaps it is as well she has taken this step. Her presence here is now no longer necessary. You have the property without the encumbrance."

Whatever Sir Ralph's opinions on the subject might have been he did not express them; but in his inmost heart he wished that she had remained under his roof, for time, he thought, would cause her to change her mind, and think more favorably of his suit, and once his wife, she could not give evidence against him should the affair of the stolen will ever come to her knowledge. He distrusted his partner in crime, and avoided as much as possible being left alone with her.

In the Bartons Edith found true friends, Julia and Emily doing everything in their power to render her stay with them as agreeable as possible. The pretty Mrs. Horace, who, from the first, had taken a great interest in her, now felt a real desire to serve one who, by the force of circumstances over which she had no control, had been left, as it were, alone in the world, and that, too, at an age and with such personal attractions as usually require the most careful watching of parent or guardian, and it entered her pretty head that she could serve her friend most effectually and at the same time secure for herself that which was so much needed in her Indian home in the far East, a personal friend and companion. Good, easy Horace, she knew, would not object, and scarcely had Edith been one week at the Willows before she had unfolded to her the scheme she had worked out for their mutual benefit; and meeting the approval of the whole family, Edith was only too happy to accompany Mrs. Barton on her return to Calcutta, for, thought she, I have no relative in England to miss me, or mourn for me, but in India I perhaps have, and her thoughts wandered to Arthur Carlton and the probability of their meeting in the land beyond the seas. After a few weeks' longer residence in Devonshire, the pretty little wife of the Judge, accompanied by Edith, left by the overland route to return to her home in the City of Palaces. And such was the effect on Edith of change of scene and a life so entirely new to her, among a people whose habits, manners and customs were strangely at variance with anything she had hitherto experienced, and she now remembered, with feelings of emotion softened by time, that uncle, whose death she had so deeply lamented, that her health and spirits gradually returned, and with them that beauty, which had adorned her before her sad bereavement, and for a few years her residence in India was in no way distasteful to her. During this time she had frequently heard of Arthur Carlton, but they had only met twice, his regiment being employed at so great a distance from Calcutta in settling some disturbances among the Rohillas of Rohilcund, that it was very difficult for a subaltern to obtain leave of absence.

A few weeks after her return, Mrs. Barton had written to Arthur, acquainting him with the fact of Edith's being in the country, and certain circumstances connected with the death of Sir Jasper Coleman, and wound up by giving him a special invitation to Chowringee for a few weeks. This she had done out of kindness to Edith, for she had some suspicion of how that young lady might be influenced by the presence of the playmate of her childhood.

Carlton received this intelligence with the utmost astonishment. He had been in complete ignorance of the Baronet's death and the changes that had taken place at Vellenaux. His last two letters to Edith had remained unanswered, or at least he had not received them. But he little knew that Mrs. Fraudhurst had taken possession of the post bag and abstracted therefrom Edith's letters to him as well as those he had sent to her. She had some apprehensions that he might contrive to make his appearance at Vellenaux at a time it was least expected or desired by either herself or Sir Ralph Coleman. His next feeling was that of joy at the thought of again meeting her, and at the idea that she was to remain in the same country perhaps for several years. As has been mentioned before, no direct words of love had passed between them, and it was not until the mighty ocean had divided them that he had realized how dear she was to him, or the strength or depth of his love for her. In his heart he secretly rejoiced that Sir Jasper's estate had passed into other hands, for what chance had he, a poor Lieutenant of Dragoons, in aspiring to the hand of the beautiful Edith, heiress of Vellenaux.

He lost no time in procuring the required furlough, and at their first meeting, the four missing letters were commented upon, and their non-delivery ascribed to the right party, namely, Mrs. Fraudhurst, as they wandered together down the pomegranate and orange groves in the cool of the evening, or pacing the broad, open verandah beneath the star lit sky.

"I think, Carlton, you must be in high feather with the Colonel, or your lucky star is in the ascendant," said Captain Hastings to our young hero, a few days after his return from Calcutta, as they rode home from stables together.

"How so? What is in the mind now?" enquired Arthur, as he reined his horse nearer to that of his companion.

"Why, there is another row among those fellows in Bundlecund, and a squadron of our regiment has been ordered out. My troop and yours have been selected for the business, and as your Captain is in Europe and the other two troop commanders absent from headquarters, you are to have charge on, this occasion. I command the squadron, so they may look out for hard knocks if we get a chance at them. I will teach the blackguards a lesson they will not forget for some time. They will find no philanthropy or mistaken clemency about me, and to tell you the truth, I would rather have you for my second in command than either Dalzell or Harcly."

"Many thanks for your good opinion; and depend upon it I shall not be backward in proving its correctness, should an opportunity offer," responded Arthur, as they entered the mess room.

The affair in Bundlecund proved a more obstinate contest than had been at first expected, and lasted for a considerable time. But the coolness and determination of the light Dragoons were too much for them, consequently the disturbance was quelled, but not before a large number of the rascals had been made to bite the dust. Here, as in Chillianwalla, Carlton's bravery and skill, as a troop leader, were conspicuous, and he well merited the encomiums that were poured upon him by his brother officers on the return of the squadron from the disturbed districts, now in a tranquil state.

# CHAPTER VIII.

Such of our readers as may have been acquainted with the West end of London some thirty-five years since, must recollect old Cavendish Square. Prior to that date it had been very exclusive, but on Belgravia and Tybernia springing into existence, the nobility and aristocratic families moved from there to the new suburban localities, and their old quarters were occupied by quite a different class, which had migrated principally from that region east of Temple Bar, such as merchants, bankers, eminent barristers, and physicians of first standing. One of the main avenues leading from this square westward, and known as Harley Street, was inhabited by another set, usually styled very respectable people, chiefly consisting of maiden ladies of doubtful ages, who kept their carriages and lived in good style, whist playing dowagers, who kept their carriages but hired job horses, when it was necessary to visit their friends whose circumstances were more flourishing than their own, and the families of country members who usually remained in town daring the session of Parliament, and often for a much longer period. It was in this street and in this circle that the Cotterells lived and moved. Mr. Cotterell, the father of Kate—the prettiest Kate in all that locality, at least, so Tom Barton said, and he ought to know for he had seen her often, and never failed to get his face as close to hers as possible whenever a chance presented itself for his so doing—was a retired stock broker who, having made a considerable hit in a great speculation by which he realized a handsome sum, prudently took the advice of his spouse and let well enough alone, retired from business, left their dusky residence in the city, and moved to their present abode, No. 54 Upper Harley Street. Mrs. Cotterell was the youngest sister of Mrs. Barton of the Willows, in Devonshire, hence the relationship between our friend, Tom Barton, and pretty cousin Kate, the charm of whose gay and lively manners had made quite an impression on the susceptible heart of cousin Tom, which increased and strengthened during the frequent visits of that young lady to her aunt's in Devonshire. Nor was it a one sided affair, for she had been captivated by the handsome person and agreeable address of her cousin, but being petit in stature, she was like most little beauties, very arbitrary and capricious towards her lover, yet, with all this, she was a girl of good, sound sense, and knowing that her portion on the death of her parents would be but small, would not consent to entangle herself in the meshes of matrimony until Tom had established himself in his profession, and there was a fair prospect of their succeeding in life.

It will be remembered that Tom Barton left for London about the same time that Arthur Carlton started for India. He had been more fortunate than could have been expected in the profession he had chosen, for he had scarcely been three years turning over musty deeds, copying legal documents and other drudgeries appertaining to a lawyer's office, when his employer died, leaving him the business and recommending him to the notice of his clients generally. Now, although Tom's chambers were situated in Lincoln's Inn Fields which everybody knows (who knows anything of London) is a large, airy space, surrounded with iron railings, wherein there are plenty of trees, flowers, grasses, and gravel walks to stroll about in, all of which could be seen from his chamber window. But this was not sufficient for him. He wanted something more suburban and evidently considered the atmosphere north of Oxford street more conducive to his health, or he would never have imposed upon himself the task of walking from Lincoln's Inn so far westward up Harley Street. Yet, although the air must have been more pure some half a mile further on, he never by any chance, succeeded in getting beyond No. 54.

There was also another gentleman who found it convenient and agreeable to walk in the same direction and stop at the same house. This for some time perplexed our friend, Tom, and gave him considerable uneasiness in the region of the heart. His first business was to discover who he was; this did not take long to accomplish, but he was more puzzled than ever; there was no one ill at No. 54, and the gentleman turned out to be a physician of good standing, residing in Cavendish Square. He dared not speak to Kate on the subject, for fear of committing himself and becoming exposed to that little lady's raillery, for he well knew that she would torment him unmercifully if he betrayed the least sign of jealousy. Wishing to be satisfied on a point that so troubled him, he determined to sound his aunt on the matter. He was a great favourite with her, and she was not likely to betray him to his lady love.

"Very quiet, gentlemanly sort of person, Doctor Ashburnham; don't you think so," he enquired of his aunt one evening, as they were seated alone in the drawing room on Harley Street?

"It is well that you are that way of thinking, for he has the same opinion of you," remarked Mrs. Cotterell with a quiet smile. "Do you remember to have met him anywhere but in London?" she asked, after a few moments' pause.

Tom shook his head and replied, "I think not, but perhaps I may have seen him somewhere. I meet all sorts of people."

"Well, well, your sister Julia is coming up to town some evening next week, and she is such a clever girl, perhaps she can enlighten you on the subject."

Tom stared at his aunt for a moment, then the mist began to clear away. It now struck him that he had never met the Doctor in Harley Street except during the time that his sister was on a visit there, and it also occurred to him now, that on his last flying visit to Devonshire he had met a gentleman much resembling Doctor Ashburnham, riding with Julia in one of the green lanes in Vellenaux. It was all clear enough now, it was Julia's lover who had given him so much concern of late, and this fact removed a great load from Tom's heart. On this discovery his face brightened up. "But, my dear aunt, is there really anything in it."

"Anything in what?" enquired the good lady, looking up from her knitting, somewhat amused at the manner in which her nephew had put the question.

"Why, I mean, is there any love affair, engagement or that sort of thing between Julia and the Doctor?"

"Well, Tom, all I can say is, that Doctor Ashburnham seldom calls here except during the time your sister is in London, or occasionally pays us a visit to enquire when she is likely to be in town again. They have met, I believe, in Devonshire, and he has visited her at the Willows. He is certainly very attentive to her when she is with us, and she appears to be anything but indifferent to his addresses; you can draw your own conclusions from that, but, as I before stated, she will be here next week and then, perhaps, she may take you into her confidence. I can say no more on the matter."

"By George! I hope it is as you say. It would be a capital match for her. He has a first rate practice, keeps quite a stylish turn out, and occupies a handsome house in Cavendish Square. I must become more intimate with him, and see if I cannot worm out exactly what he is driving at." Here Tom took his hat, and started down stairs three steps at a time, nearly upsetting the Doctor in the hall in his great hurry. "Beg pardon, my dear sir, quite accidental I assure you; in haste to speak to Mr. Cotterell in the library," said Tom apologetically.

"Don't mention it, pray, Mr. Barton," was the reply, as that gentleman quickly ascended the staircase leading to the drawing room.

Now, Tom really had no business with Mr. Cotterell that evening, nor would he have intruded on that worthy person, but for his encounter with the Doctor. He would, he thought, not remain long with his aunt, and it would be a good opportunity to push his enquiries, could he but manage to go out with him. His anticipations proved correct. The Doctor did not remain long up stairs, and our friend Tom managed to meet him again as he was passing through the hall.

"Fine evening, sir; which way are you walking?" said Tom, seeing no vehicle in attendance.

"I am returning to Cavendish Square, sir," was the ready reply.

"I also am going in that direction, and if you have no objection will walk with you," returned Tom Barton. The two gentlemen walked together, chatting in a very friendly way on the different topics of the day until they had reached the door of the Doctor's residence, when that gentleman surprised Tom by saying, "Mr. Barton, will you do me the favor to step in for a few moments? I wish to speak to you on a subject that cannot very well be discussed in the public street." Nothing loath, Tom agreed and was ushered into a very snug apartment, half library, half smoking divan.

"You smoke, of course," said the Doctor, pointing at the same time to an array of pipes and tobacco of different kinds on a small side table. Fill, then, drop into that easy chair, and I will tell you why I have requested you to enter my snuggery. Tom acted upon his suggestion, and was soon sending great puffs of smoke half way across the room. His host followed this very laudable example, and after a few whiffs, at once opened the business by candidly, and in a straightforward, manner, telling Tom the great love and admiration he felt for Miss Barton, whom he had frequently met in Devonshire as well as in London, and that he had vanity enough to believe that his love was reciprocated, and declared his intention on Julia's arrival to decide the affair by making her an offer of his hand and heart, and finished by requesting Tom to forward his views to the best of his ability.

To this Tom readily assented. "The sly little puss," he continued, "not to mention a word of it even to me. But I suppose it is not considered by the fair sex quite the thing to speak to any one on so delicate a subject until after the gentleman has popped the question." Shortly after, he took his departure for his chambers at Lincoln's Inn, and it was noticed that Doctor Ashburnham and Mr. Tom Barton were seen more frequently together than had hitherto been the case.

Miss Barton arrived, as had been expected by her relatives in Harley Street, and the physician from Cavendish Square called there every day, although there was no illness or epidemic in the house, save that known as the heart disease, and so earnestly did the Doctor press his suit that Julia must have been hard-hearted indeed to have refused to add to his happiness by encumbering him with a wife, and ere she returned to Devonshire, it was finally settled that the wedding was to take place at the end of the following month, and a very dashing affair it proved. The lawn sleeves at Saint George's, Hanover Square, were called into requisition on the occasion. There was a great display of white corded silk, lace orange blossoms, muslins and wreaths of white roses. Gunter, of Berkly square, was called upon to supply a wedding breakfast, which was partaken of at the Cotterells', and after some champagne had been drank, and the speeches usual on the occasion made, the happy pair started on their wedding tour through the South of England, calling, of course, at the Willows on their way. After visiting Scotland they returned to London, and settled comfortably down to the humdrum of every day life in the Doctor's handsome establishment in Cavendish Square, which had been re-decorated and furnished for them during their absence.

Not many months elapsed before the happiness of our young friends was somewhat over-shadowed by the death of the worthy old couple at the Willows, who expired within two months of each other. Mr. Barton died of old age, and his wife from influenza, caught while attending church to hear the funeral sermon.

Horace Barton not being expected in England for some time, the Willows was let on a short lease, and Emily came up to London to reside with her aunt in Harley Street, occasionally spending several weeks with her sister, Mrs. Ashburnham.

Our young lawyer was slowly but surely increasing his practice. He had used all his powers of persuasion to induce Kate to allow him to lead her to the altar on the same day that his sister was married, but in vain, for that young lady declared that she would rather take a second class character in the interesting tableau this time, with the view of being better able to sustain the role of the principal actress in a similar pageant at some future time. With this decision Tom had to remain satisfied for the present and attend to business. But in the course of time circumstances transpired which prevented him from attaining any eminence as a lawyer. A distant relative of Mr. Cotterell's and Godmother to Kate, departed this life, leaving her Godchild the very comfortable sum of six hundred per annum, secured in the four per cents., and after wearing mourning for a suitable period, Kate took the initiative by announcing to Tom, very much to his surprise and delight, that she was both ready and willing to become his wife on the following conditions, which were, that he should give up practising law, take a snug cottage in Devonshire, and turn his attention to haymaking, shooting, &c, and retire from London life altogether, for she said that in the country they could live very comfortably on six hundred a year and be thought somebodies, but they could scarcely exist in London on that sum and then be thought nobodies.

If our young lawyer had any scruples on the score of giving up his profession and thereby losing all chance of ever attaining to the dignity of Lord Chancellor, he certainly kept them to himself, for he had no wish to run counter to the inclination of Kate, or he might find himself in the position of the dog in the fable, who had thrown away the substance to endeavour to grasp the shadow. Tom, in reality, had never liked a London life, and had a constant hankering after field sports, shooting and fishing; and now he believed he could indulge in these to the top of his bent. They could live very comfortably on their joint income, for he had received a certain sum on the death of his parents, and likewise made something during the past few years by his profession, which he had increased by placing it out at interest. Moreover, he knew exactly where to find a house and grounds that would suit them; the very one that Kate had so admired during their strolls around

Vellenaux. It was picturesquely situated in a shady dell, through which ran a flowing brook which deepened and widened as it flowed on towards the sea, and was the favourite resort of the angler and amateur fisherman—about an equal distance from the Willows and the Rectory, and but a short walk from the woods and park of Vellenaux. There were Horace's grounds to shoot over, and although Sir Ralph Coleman was not a neighbour best suited to his taste, yet he felt certain that he would not object to his occasionally using his preserves, or bagging a few brace of birds on his turnip fields. All this, together with a pretty little loving wife for a companion, was, to Tom's notion, something worth living for, and a position he would not exchange for all the gaieties of London life with a seat on the woolsack into the bargain.

Again No. 54 Harley Street was thrown into a state of bustle and confusion. Millinery girls, with innumerable band boxes, and oddly shaped parcels were continually arriving. In the drawing room there was assembled daily a sort of joint high commission, consisting of a bevy of pretty maidens with one or two handsome matrons, who were engaged in deciding on the colour, material, and cut of certain wearables appertaining to the wedding trousseau of Miss Cotterell. There were continual visits made to the fashionable emporiums of silk, lace &c., in Oxford and Regent streets, and other parts of the metropolis. The wedding day at length arrived. A considerable distance up Harley Street was lined with carriages of various descriptions, the coachmen and footmen of which appeared in holiday costume and wearing white satin favors, and there was quite an excitement in the immediate vicinity to witness the arrival and departure of the wedding party to and from church. Kate Cotterell, attended by her six bridesmaids all looking very lovely in toilettes befitting the occasion, created quite a sensation among the spectators as they stepped from No. 54 into the carriages that were to convey them to Hanover Square.

After a very *recherche* breakfast, served in Gunter's best style, in the handsome drawing room of the Cotterells', in Harley Street, Tom and his fair bride took their departure *en route* for the Continent. They were to make a tour of several months through France, Germany and Switzerland, likewise enjoy several weeks on the banks of the beautiful Rhine.

Mr. Cotterell undertook to arrange matters concerning the purchase of the cottage so much admired, which he intended to present to his daughter as a marriage gift, and aunt Sarah, Emily, and Mrs. Ashburnham took upon themselves the responsibility of furnishing the said cottage, and otherwise rendering it in every way suitable for the reception of the happy couple, and thus enable them to commence housekeeping immediately on their return to England.

The various events and proceedings were duly recorded and forwarded from time to time for the information of Horace and Pauline Barton, in their Eastern home on the banks of the Hoogly; and Edith, who still kept up a correspondence with Kate and Julia, received a full account, descriptive of the wedding trousseaus and paraphernalia incident to both ceremonies, and followed up by a delicate enquiry as to when she intended to return the compliment by favouring them with the details of an Indian wedding, which they supposed must soon take place, and would, no doubt, prove a gorgeous and magnificent affair in true oriental style. So wrote the happy girls to their old friend and companion in Calcutta, for, according to Pauline's account, she had no end of suitors among the wealthiest in the land.

To all those enquiries Edith's usual reply was that the time was somewhat distant when she could indulge in dreams of happiness. Her position was somewhat changed, thus, probably, the event they so often alluded to might never take place, and the reader must remember, that although Edith and Arthur were, beyond doubt, devotedly attached to each other, the word that would have made them both happy had not yet been spoken; there was no engagement, or in fact, any advance towards one, yet both, in their heart of hearts, realized the great love they felt for each other. But prudential motives had kept Arthur silent. Edith knew this and was content to wait for the developments of the future. In the meantime she did not hesitate to participate in the amusements and enjoyments which offered, and which were continually pressed upon her by her kind friends, the Bartons.

# CHAPTER IX.

The capital of Bengal was a very gay city. What with balls and public breakfasts at the Governor General's, brilliant assemblages given by the Civil Service Granders, with no end of picnics, theatricals, cricket matches and races improvised by the military and naval officers, for the especial benefit (at least so they said) of the beautiful, gay butterflies that condescended to grace, with their presence, such assemblages; and Pauline Barton never allowed these occurrences to transpire without inducing the beautiful Miss Effingham, as she was usually styled, to accompany her, for Pauline was, indeed, very popular in Chowringee and around its vicinity, and her Bungalow was a constant lounge for the gallants of all services. Horace was no niggard in his hospitality, but preferred the ease and comfort of his own sanctum to the gay rattle that was continually going on in his pretty little wife's drawing room or verandahs. And Arthur was again, for a fourth time since his arrival in the country, in Calcutta. He had contrived to get appointed one of a committee for the purchasing of troop horses for his regiment and this would detain him at the Presidency for a couple of months. This was a source of much pleasure to Edith, for sometimes accompanied by Mrs. Barton, but more frequently alone, would Arthur and Edith, either driving or on horseback, wend their way through the shaded avenues that crossed the Midan, along the strand by the river side to Garden, reach and loiter in the Botanical Gardens; this being considered by the Grandees the most fashionable resort for a canter in the early morn or a pleasant drive about sunset.

It never entered the head of pretty Mrs. Barton that there could be any serious love making between her friend and the handsome Lieutenant. She knew that they had been brought up together from childhood and were more like brother and sister than lovers, and had such an idea been suggested to her by any of her friends, she would have pooh poohed it as mere moonshine. She knew that it was out of the question for a Subaltern to enter the matrimonial arena; besides the brilliant beauty of Miss Effingham must command a suitable alliance and an enviable position whenever she cared to enter upon the responsibility of married life, and it appeared evident that Edith was in no hurry to take the initiative or allow herself to be led away by the flattering speeches she daily heard from those, by whom she was surrounded. Nor was Mrs. Barton at all desirous that she should enter into any such engagement, for she was well aware that it was the charm of her fair friend's manner that drew to her house the most agreeable and handsomest men of the capital. She knew likewise that it was Horace's intention to settle in England as soon as his term of service should expire, and it would then be time for Edith to select from her numerous admirers the one she most preferred, but until that time she should be exceedingly sorry to part with her.

"Do you intend spending the day at Mrs. Deborah's?" enquired Mrs. Barton of Edith as they rose from the breakfast table. Edith replied in the affirmative. "Well, then, I will send the palkee for you; but do not be late, my dear, for dinner." She had no intention of being too late, as she knew that in all probability Arthur would make his appearance during the evening. The distance from the Bartons to her friend's Bungalow was not more than half a mile. The road lay through a very picturesque but somewhat lonely part of the suburbs. The Date and stately Palms, intermingled with the blossom of the gold Mohur trees, looked so very lovely by the light of the setting sun. For some cause or other Edith's palkee did not arrive at the time appointed, and not wishing to trouble her friend—who usually sent her children at sunset in their palkee for an airing—and attracted by the beauty of the scene, she started to walk home, thinking of the pleasure of meeting Arthur. Her mind was engaged on this subject when she reached a Date grove, a short distance from the road side, and so busy was she with her thoughts, she had not noticed that for the past few minutes she had been followed by a tall, burly mussulman, and he came upon her before she was aware of his presence. Without a word of warning, he threw his long arms around her waist, and endeavored to drag or carry her to the Date grove. There could be no mistaking his intentions, and he would no doubt have succeeded in carrying out his villainous design—for the terrified girl was in a half fainting condition, and unable from the suddenness of the attack, to offer much resistance—when Arthur Carlton, who had been attracted to the spot by her shrieks and cries for help, came to the rescue. He had called at the Bungalow, and learning where she might be found, had set out in search of her, and arrived just in time. The ruffian managed to make good his escape, not, however, before he had received several marks of Arthur's favor from the horsewhip he carried. He then supported the still, trembling girl home, and she soon forgot, in his society, the danger which had menaced her.

Exasperated beyond measure at so rare an occurrence as the attack made on his beloved Edith, he at once sought the aid of the police, and from the description given they soon succeeded in tracing the offender, who proved to be a Subaltern of the native cavalry. The affair was reported to head quarters, and a court of enquiry was summoned which resulted in the court martial and dismissal from service of the blackguard, who immediately left the station, vowing to have his revenge on Carlton, should ever an opportunity occur for so doing, and this, with a Mahammedan means mischief, for they never rest in their endeavors to effect a purpose.

The duties which brought Carlton to Calcutta were now at an end, and the Lieutenant had to return to head quarters. Edith, being of an enquiring turn of mind, acquired a great deal of information respecting the natives' character, their castes, customs and ceremonies, and by the aid of a Moonshee soon learned to speak with ease and fluency the Hindostan language. This she turned to account in the management of the household servants.

Calcutta is the largest city in British India, and is situated on the bank of the Hoogley, one of the branches of the river Ganges, held as sacred by the natives. There are quite a number of Europeans and professing Christians, numbering in the aggregate about fourteen thousand, the principal portions of which are half castes, three quarter castes, Euroasians, Portuguese and Hindoo Britons. The half castes are the progeny of the European men and native women. The three-quarter-castes, that of European fathers and half-caste mothers. The Euroasians spring from European and three-quarter-caste parents, while the Hindoo Britons are the children of European parents, born in India. The Portuguese likewise intermarry with these classes. These people make up the principal number of those professing Christianity throughout the Presidency. The churches of England, Rome, and Scotland were well attended by the officers of the civil service, army and navy, with their families, among which there is very little sectarianism. But the Roman Catholic faith is largely diffused among the other classes. The native population of all castes number about six hundred thousand, and although they have no regular Sunday or day of rest, they have quite a number of religious festivals or holidays which they scrupulously observe.

The principal festival, and the one most religiously kept of all the holidays among the true believers—as the followers of Mahomet style themselves—is that of the Moharum, which lasts ten days, commencing from the appearance of the new moon, in the month of November, during which time handsome temples and mosques are constructed of bamboo and paper, and embellished with glass, paint and gilding. On the last day they are carried in grand procession through the public thoroughfares, proceeded by a band of music and accompanied by an immense concourse of spectators. Many of the faithful prostrate themselves before these Taboots, and in many instances rolling over and over in the muddy streets for a considerable distance, being generally well primed with bang or opium. There are occasional disturbances between the fanatics of the different castes, for many of these work themselves up to a pitch of frenzy by the use of narcotics and other stimulants, but the Government always take steps to prevent any serious outbreak, by having the troops posted in different parts of the town, ready to turn out at a moment's notice, and a strong body of police mounted and on foot accompany the procession to enforce order. At sunset they reach the river, and the day's proceedings terminate by the Taboots being thrown into the water, amid the shouts, gesticulation and vociferations of the now thoroughly excited populace.

The Dewally Festival is equally recognized by natives of all castes and denominations as a sort of New Year's Day. Accounts for the past year are closed, and new books are opened. The dirt and rubbish of the past twelvemonth is removed, the houses thoroughly cleansed and at night the city or town is illuminated with lamps, Chinese lanterns, and other descriptions of lights, and the houses thrown open for general hospitality.

The Hooley, the most revolting of all Hindoo Festivals, draws together an immense concourse of people. Large fires are made on the sides of the public streets and liquid dye stuffs, with every description of filth is thrown by the Hindoos on each other, and should any unfortunate Hindoo woman show herself in the street on these occasions, she is assaulted with language of the most obscene and disgusting nature. These festivals have of late years been curtailed by the Government, and now seldom last more than two days—that is, in large cities containing European communities—but in native towns it is still of many days duration.

Accounts of these and other native ceremonies, together with the horrors of the black hole, experienced by Europeans, nearly one hundred years since at the suggestion of the native princes, had been related to Edith by her Moonshee Ayah, but their dominion, or power for good or evil, has now passed away, and Calcutta of the present day is one of the pleasantest and finest cities to the European to be found throughout our Indian possessions.

And were it not for the great change in her position, from absolute affluence to becoming the recipient of another's bounty, Edith would have been, if not quite happy, at least contented. Yet it must not be imagined that she was ungrateful or the less thankful to her kind protectors, the Bartons, for she could now well realize what might have been her situation had she been compelled to act upon the plan that had first suggested itself to her on leaving Vellenaux—that of becoming a governess or companion to some antiquated Dowager in Europe.

The repeated assurances from Mrs. Barton that she would, at no distant period, secure a brilliant alliance, fell coldly on her ear, but she made no ostentative demonstration of her own ideas on the subject, but with a gentle and quiet dignity, repelled the advances of certain aspirants for her hand, who were continually to be found in her train whenever she appeared abroad. She had a smile for all and a fascinating and bewitching manner which was equally bestowed among her would-be admirers. But beyond this all was calm and cold. Her heart had imperceptibly slipped from her, and was now in the care of another, nor would she wish it were otherwise. The future was before her and she was willing to wait.

Let it not be imagined that Arthur Carlton was a lukewarm lover, coldly prudential, or thinking it would be time enough to marry when he should have obtained his Captaincy, and careless as to what trying position Edith might be placed in, surrounded, as he knew her to be, by those who would willingly wed her at any moment. Far from it. He loved her too well to ask her to share at present the inconveniences incident to a camp life, as experienced by the wives of subalterns, not that he doubted she would yield up without a single regret the gay society and splendid establishment of Mrs. Barton, and contentedly share with him his home, be it ever so humble. But the thought of her having to make any such sacrifice was to him one that could not be entertained for a moment. He believed he knew her sufficiently well to trust implicitly in her constancy, and await the happy time when he could in all honour formally propose for her hand.

About a twelvemonth prior to the outbreak of the great Sepoy mutiny, it pleased the authorities to change the scene of Mr. Barton's labors from Chowringee, that Belgravia of Calcutta, to Goolampore, a military station of some importance in the northwest provinces, or more properly speaking in the Goozeratte country. This act of the Government, although particularly objectionable to Mrs. Barton, was exactly what her lord and master desired. His term of service would shortly come to a close, and therefore, in his opinion, it became expedient, not only to retrench his expenses, which he could not do at the gay Capitol, but likewise gather in a few more of the loaves and fishes of office, which were said to be found in greater abundance at a distance from the seat of Government, besides Mr. Barton was in the decline of life, and felt that the harness of office life did not fit so easily upon him while under the immediate supervision of the Suddur Aydowlett, as it would do when removed from its immediate influence. However, be this as it may, he was quite content with the change, nor was he the only one to whom this change was a sort of relief. The City of Palaces and its surroundings had become distasteful to Edith; not that she disliked the Capitol or the pleasures to be found there; but she felt wearied and annoyed by the attentions that were showered upon her by the numerous suitors who thronged around her, using all the powers of persuasion they had at command, to induce her to listen to their respective suits. The parchment visaged Nabob, with his sacks of rupees, the wealthy planter, whose fortune had been wrung from either opium or indigo, perhaps both, the rich civil servant and field officer, with numerous others, all jostling and hedging each other in the race for the hand of the beautiful Miss Effingham; but the prize was not for them. She cared not a jot for either their persons or their purses and would not consent to be caught, and like a bird in a golden cage, flutter without the means of escape.

But there was one for whom she did care, one whose image was indelibly stamped on her heart, and whom she loved as woman only can love, and this favored one was Arthur Carlton, Lieut. H.M. Light Dragoons—the playmate of her childhood, and companion of her riper years in the golden days at Vellenaux, in dear old England.

"It is absurd in the directors, or whoever has to do with it, to send Horace off to the Northwest, just at the commencement of the season too; besides, we shall scarcely be settled before we shall have to return to England. I declare we are being treated shamefully," said Mrs. Barton, as she stepped from the Chuppaul Ghat to the Budgerow that was to convey them to the steamer, in which a passage had been provided by the Government for them, to the nearest port on the coast of Goozeratte, *en route* for Goolampore, "and to think," again resumed the little lady to Edith, as they sat together in the handsomely furnished cabin, "that your brilliant prospects will be destroyed; for who is there in the interior that will compensate for the loss of those eligible suitors for your hand?" Edith disclaimed against brilliant alliances or the admirers referred to.

"It is all very fine, my dear, for you to say so; but depend upon it, for a young lady in your position and circumstances, there is nothing equal to a wealthy husband, and an establishment of your own. But what I shall do without you I really do not know; but I expect it must come to that some day or other." Here the good lady sank back among her cushions, and resigned herself to her fate, her Ayah, and her last new novel.

For several months all went pleasantly enough with the Bartons, much more so, indeed than had been anticipated by her little ladyship; for she found that as wife of the judge, the highest civil functionary in the station, she was leader of fashion, and took precedence of all other ladies in Goolampore; and Edith, for a time, found herself relieved from the importunities that beset her at Calcutta. Not that she lacked admirers, but certainly at present their attentions were not sufficiently marked to give her any annoyance.

The worthy judge was retrenching. His expenses were scarcely one fourth of what they had been at the Presidency. He had attained his object, and all things for the time being *couleur de rose*.

"Come here pretty one," said he as he noticed Edith dismounting, after her usual ride around the race course and band stand, one beautiful evening. "Listen! here is something in the papers that will greatly interest you, or I am much mistaken." Edith was soon at his side, all attention, when the gentleman proceeded to read as follows:—"Extract from general orders. His Excellency the Commander in Chief has been pleased to appoint Lieutenant Arthur Carlton, H.M. Light Dragoons, to act as A.D.C. on the staff of General D——, at Goolampore. That officer will proceed and assume his duties at that station forthwith." Edith could not conceal her joy at this unexpected event, and retired to her chamber in a flutter of agitation, but happier in heart than she had been for many months past.

It was the anniversary of Her Majesty's birthday, and, as was customary at all military stations, it was celebrated by a military display in the morning, theatricals, and a supper and ball at night. The Assembly rooms, as they were called at Goolampore, were built by Government. It was a building of considerable length, divided into three rooms, eighty feet long, by forty feet wide. The end one was fitted up in very handsome style as a theatre, the other two communicating with it by means of enormous folding doors, and were used on ordinary occasions by the military department for holding courts martial, courts of enquiry, committees, &c. The other was at the disposal of the political agents or chief magistrate to transact such business as they might deem necessary. But on such occasions as the present, or others of a similar character, the whole three were brilliantly illuminated and thrown open for the amusement of the *elite* of the station.

"I say Hopkins, as you know everything and everybody, tell me, who is that young fellow in staff uniform, dancing with Miss Effingham?" enquired a Colonel of the N.I.

"That is young Carlton of the Dragoons, the new A.D.C. He only arrived this morning. Capital fellow I am told; a tip top sportsman; goes in strong for tiger shooting and all that kind of game," was the reply.

"He appears to go in—as you call it—pretty strong for another description of game. Why, this is the third time he has danced with that young lady. Rather strong, that, I should say for a first introduction," responded the Colonel, about to move off, when his friend continued:

"Oh, they are old acquaintances. I met him at the Bartons this afternoon, where he appeared quite at home, turning over the music and accompanying *la belle*, Edith, in one of her favourite songs, apparently very much to each others satisfaction. But the next waltz is about to commence," said Captain Hopkins, "and I must claim my partner," and the man who knew everything and everybody was soon waltzing with great assiduity.

"You will allow me the pleasure of attending you in your morning and evening rides, whenever my duties will admit of it, dear Edith," whispered Arthur as he handed her to the carriage at the close of the festivities. With a sweet smile the promise was given, and the carriage whirled off.

The new A.D.C. soon became a general favourite. Courteous and gentlemanly in the drawing room, and ever ready to attend the ladies *en cavalier*, he could not fail to win the esteem of the fair sex. He was a first-class swordsman, a bold rider, and a keen sportsman; therefore held in great repute by his companions in arms. He had scoured the jungles for thirty miles around Goolampore, and knew the haunts of the tiger and cheetah better than any man in the station. This was proved by the numerous trophies in the shape of skins and heads that he brought in. So our young friend, basking in the smiles of beauty, and especially of hers whom he loved so well, was consequently envied by others less fortunate in this respect than himself; and in this delightful manner weeks passed away. But dark clouds were rising in the distance which were gradually closing around them to destroy the tranquility of the station.

# CHAPTER X.

Reports began to arise of the disloyalty and insubordination of some of the native regiments; but at first little notice was taken of the circumstance, it being believed that the rumours were greatly exaggerated, and that, if there was anything really in it, the matter would soon be put to rights by the Government, either by proclamation or by force of arms. But report followed report and the mutiny continued, when the massacre at Cawnpore took place, and the affair at Lucknow, and the horrors enacted at the Star Fort of Jansee, where the officer commanding, after doing everything that could be done to protect the unfortunate inmates, just as the mutineers were in the act of bursting open the gates, well knowing what would be the result should they fall into the hands of the remorseless natives, with his own hand shot his wife and child, and then deliberately blew out his own brains. Those who were captured met a death so horrible and revolting at the hands of and under the immediate supervision of that incarnate fiend and she devil, the Rannee of Jansee, the details of which are totally unfit for publication. Then, and not till then, the magnitude of the danger was realized.

Mr. Barton, whose health had been on the decline some weeks past, and whose term of service in India nearly expired, declared that he would no longer remain in the country, and obtained leave of absence to proceed to Bombay, in anticipation of finally leaving for Europe. Mrs. Barton, always nervous, became alarmed for her personal safety, and urged their immediate departure with much vehemence, and it was arranged that they should start at once for Rutlaum *en route* for the sea coast, and that Miss Effingham should remain and see everything packed up and the servants sent on, then follow herself and overtake them at Rutlaum, where they were to make a halt for a few days. Several other families also left about the same time, for the tide of mutiny and rebellion was now sweeping like the red pestilence through the whole of the North West provinces. Mohow, Indore, Meidpoore, Mundasore, Neemuch and other places of greater or lesser note, had already become the scene of many a bloody drama and fiendish outrage. In fact, whenever native troops had been located, ruin and desolation reigned triumphant. Public edifices were thrown down, Bungalows burned and the Bazaars plundered, while helpless and unprotected Europeans, irrespective of sex or age, were seized, and after suffering the most brutal indignities, ruthlessly slaughtered by the fanatical and blood-thirsty native soldiery.

Goolampore and its immediate vicinity, up to the present period, had remained in perfect tranquility. The native mind was apparently undisturbed by the great convulsions that were now shaking, to its very centre, the supremacy of British power in India; but it was only the lull before the storm, which was so soon to burst and fall like a thunderbolt on the hitherto peaceful station.

The Brigade here consisted of the following troops: One troop of European horse artillery, one regiment of native cavalry, and two battalions of Sepoys. This force was commanded by a Brigadier of the Bengal army; but, having been on the staff for many years, was unequal to an emergency like the present, and such was his belief in the loyalty of the men under his command, that he refused to listen to the reports made to him from time to time by his staff, and others well qualified to give an opinion on the matter, until it was too late and many valuable lives had been sacrificed.

The evening was clear and calm, countless stars studded the dark purple vault of heaven. The young moon shed her silvery light o'er lake and mountain, the atmosphere was no longer influenced by the stifling heat of the scorching sun; a deliciously cool breeze wafted from the ocean that rolled into the Gulf of Cambay, and washed the shores of the Goozeratte, played and rustled among the leaves of the trees and flowers, imparting to the senses a delicious feeling of relief and delight.

In a broad and spacious verandah of the cavalry mess house were assembled a group of officers of different corps. Some stretched at full length on ottomans, enjoying the music of an excellent band; others smoking, laughing or chatting on the various events that were passing around them.

"Listen to me, gentlemen," said a tall, handsome man, about thirty, and the very *beau ideal* of a cavalry officer, who had for some time been leaning over the balustrade of the verandah, quietly puffing circles of white smoke from his cheroot, and gazing thoughtfully on the moonlit scene before him, and who had hitherto taken no part in the conversation that was going on. "This deceitful calm," said he, drawing himself up to his full height, and advancing to the centre of the group, "will not, cannot last much longer, and it is high time that something should be done for the protection of the families of the European Warrant Officers and staff, Non-Commissioned Officers and others who are residing at different parts of the station, and who would be the first to fall victims to the licentious passion and murderous designs of the troops, should an outbreak ensue before we are re-enforced by more Europeans."

"Right! Major Collingwood is right," exclaimed a Colonel of one of the Sepoy battalions; "too much valuable time has already been lost. What the deuce has come to the Brigadier? Huntingdon, of the Artillery, proposed to him to give an order for the families of the Europeans of his troop to move at once into the Fort, but he would not listen to him, stating that there was no necessity for such a course, and that he would answer for the loyalty and good behavior of the troops under his command."

"This comes of trusting the lives and property of Europeans in the care of General D—— and others of his stamp, who from a long association in a civil capacity with the natives, have become so wrapped up in them, and so hoodwinked, that they will see nothing, only through the spectacles provided for them by the native functionaries, who always toady and flatter their European masters," was the contemptuous remark of one of the party. The last speaker was here interrupted by the Brigade Major, who came bounding up the steps of the verandah, three at a time. "What is the matter, Grey?" enquired several voices at one time. "Oh! there has been the devil to pay at Headquarters, and no pitch hot," was the hasty reply of the staff officer. "Explain yourself, if you please," said Major Collingwood. "What has taken place?"

"Why Huntingdon, in spite of the Brigadier's refusal to grant permission, has sent the married people of his troop within the Fort, and detailed several troopers to man the guns, and put the place in a state of defence, in case of any sudden rising among the natives. General D—— became furious when Huntingdon told him what he had done, and threatened to arrest him. On young Carlton, the new A.D.C., taking sides with the commander of the artillery, and applauding the act, old D—— turned upon him like a lion. A violent squabble ensued, which resulted in Arthur Carlton resigning his appointment on the Staff, and expressed his determination to rejoin his regiment without delay."

"Well done, Huntingdon. That is a step in the right direction. It is a pity that the non-commissioned staff of the station could not have been included," responded several voices; and all praised the plucky way in which young Carlton had acted, though sorry to lose the services of so valuable a sabre as Arthur was known to be, especially at a time when stout hearts and bold riders were necessary to the salvation of the station.

"Pinkerton, Jones, and others acted wisely in sending their families away last week; but I do not think it was quite the thing for the Bartons to leave the pretty Miss Effingham behind to arrange their household affairs, and then make her way to Rutlaum as she best could. Who will see her there in safety?" exclaimed the staff Surgeon.

"Oh, as far as that matters, that young lady would, doubtless, have a score of volunteers to act as her escort, should she require one," said the first speaker; "but I do not think she would accept such an offer, nor do I imagine Arthur Carlton would feel obliged to any one in Goolampore for acting as her guide and protector, while he was at hand to perform so delightful a service," responded Captain Hopkins, with a light laugh, "for you must know that he has been a constant visitor at the Bartons since his arrival, and are they not always to be seen riding together at the race course and band stand? Why, he is her very shadow."

"Miss Effingham is too fine a girl, and has too much good sense to throw herself away on a penniless Lieutenant of Dragoons, when she knows that there are others of high standing in the service who are both able and willing to offer her an establishment and position in society that he will be unable to do for years to come," said a grey haired Colonel of Infantry.

"Phew!" ejaculated a young Cornet. "Sets the wind in that quarter? I wonder if the pretty Edith will be proof against three lacs of rupees? I am afraid the A.D.C.'s chances for the lady will soon sink below par; but there is no accounting for the doings of pretty women, for 'Love levels rank—lords down to cellar-bears, etc.'"

The parties now began to disperse to their various quarters. No doubt many were ruminating as to what might be the result of the fracas at the Brigadiers quarters, just related to them by the Major of Brigade.

The following morning as the Brigadier was preparing to mount his horse and take his usual ride through the cantonments, the Adjutant of one of the Sepoy battalions came up at full gallop to where he was standing, with the, (to him) astounding intelligence that, during the night, a large body of irregular horse had entered the limits of the station, visiting the cavalry and Sepoy lines, and had arranged with them to unite in plundering the Bazaar, seize the guns of the artillery, put to death all the Europeans that might oppose them, and that the men of his own corps and those of the other battalion were then in the act of breaking open the bells-of-arms and taking therefrom the muskets and ammunition.

"Phew! There must be some mistake, your fears must have misled you. The men may be somewhat excited. I will go down and reason with them—they will listen to me, for they know I am their friend"—and the General turned his horse's head in the direction of the Sepoy lines, requesting him to follow. The Adjutant replied:

"My instructions from the Colonel were to report the circumstance to you, then ride to the horse artillery and acquaint Major Huntingdon and others with it," then, saluting his superior officer, he galloped off. Bursting with indignation at the conduct of those around him, who, until the last few hours, were ready to obey without scruple any order, he might give, the General called his Brigade Major, and ordered him to ride with him. That officer shrugged his shoulders, but obeyed the command, and they rode off together. They were soon recognized by the mutineers. A hurried consultation among the native commissioned and non-commissioned officers took place. Some Were for arresting the Brigadier and his Major of Brigade, and holding them prisoners until the guns and Fort were surrendered to them; others were of a different opinion, and insisted that the two officers should be put to death. They argued that delay was dangerous; reinforcements of Europeans might arrive at any hour, and that nothing would be left for them but to make a rapid retrograde movement, and advised the immediate looting of the town. This party, being the strongest and most clamorous, carried their point; and three Sepoys thereupon leveled their muskets and fired, but without having any effect, as the bullets flew wide of their mark. But this was the signal that the irregular cavalry were so anxiously watching for, and immediately encircled the two unfortunate gentlemen who, drawing their weapons, prepared to defend their lives to the last. But what could two men do against a score of fanatical ruffians, thirsting for the blood of Christians. Some of the troopers fell from the effect of the bullets from the Brigadier's revolver, and some were severely wounded by the sabre of poor Captain Grey, but all to no purpose; they were soon overpowered and literally hewn to pieces by the sowars of the cavalry who, by this time, had been joined by the regulars. The party then started off at a canter to the artillery lines, to secure the guns and open the magazine, if they could but obtain the key from the ordinance warrant officer, while the infantry made an attempt to carry the Fort by storm; but having neither guns nor scaling ladders, they signally failed in their attempt, and suffered considerable loss from the spherical case and round shot that was hurled at them from the guns of the fort. The party, to whom fell the work of plundering the Bazaar, were, for a time, very successful, and numerous large Bungalows were soon in a blaze.

The party of cavalry, regular and irregular, who were to attempt to carry off from the magazine such ammunition as they might find, went in the direction of the place, and on their way intercepted the European ordnance conductor, who had charge of the keys, which they at once demanded, but were promptly refused by that officer, who declared he had them not, and immediately stood on the defensive; but a shot from the carbine of one of the troopers, brought him bleeding to the earth. A couple of them dismounted, and with oaths and imprecations, both loud and bitter, stripped off his uniform in search of the magazine keys, but they were not to be found. Drawing his creese, one of the villains cut the throat of the wounded man, nearly severing the head from the body. The others satisfied themselves by merely spitting upon the naked body.

"It is useless to go on without the keys," said a Havildar of the regulars. "Let us move off at once to his Bungalow, they must be there. I know the road, follow me!" and the whole party galloped off and soon reached the murdered man's quarters, where they halted and dismounted.

The terrified woman, wife of the poor fellow who had just been so savagely slaughtered, saw them approaching, and judging their intentions, bolted and barred all the doors and windows, and with her two young children, mere babes, the eldest being scarcely four years of age, retreated to a small closet in an inner room, and locked the door. For some time the troopers, who had now worked themselves up to a pitch of frenzy, could not effect an entrance: but at length, tearing down one of the wooden uprights of the verandah, used it as a sort of ram, and soon battered down the door. Then, with a yell of triumph, rushed into the house, searched every nook and corner far what they so much wished to find, smashing and destroying everything that came in their way, but they were doomed to disappointment. A bullet from one of their holster pistols blew the lock from the door of the closet, and the poor mother and her helpless babes were seized and dragged forth by these monsters in human form. The mother was brutally outraged, and her clothing torn and stripped from her person. A large empty chest, which usually contained clothing, caught the attention of one of the number, and a fiendish thought flashed through his mind, which he communicated to some of the others, and they proceeded to carry it out. Collecting the broken furniture, bed linen, etc., they made a large fire and placed the box in question thereon; then tossed the helpless children into it and literally roasted them alive in the presence of the agonized mother, who made frantic attempts to break from her captors, and rescue her offspring, but it was in vain; they held her firmly until the chest and its contents were reduced to embers; then two of them plunged their creeses into her naked bosom, and flung her bleeding body into the fire to be consumed like those of her children. Other enormities were being enacted in various parts of Goolampore during the short time the mutineers remained there. But an act of unparalleled atrocity was perpetuated on the Postmaster and his wife, who, it appears, had, on the morning in question, gone to look at their new Bungalow which was in course of erection in the suburbs, when they were pounced upon by a body of Sepoys, who were making good their exodus from the station, having no desire to come in contact with the horse artillery, the booming of whose guns sounded not at all pleasantly in their ears. These inhuman wretches dashed at their victims and, after tormenting them almost to madness by their devilish cruelties, dragged them to a sawpit, where pieces of square timber, which had been partially cut into planks for building purposes, lay. The unhappy pair were then bound on two separate planks, then another plank was placed on the top of each, and tightly bound together with strips of fine bamboo; the monsters laughing and gesticulating at what they termed the living sandwiches, dainty morsels to be offered up as a sacrifice to their Deities. The crowning act of this fearful drama was at last enacted by the remorseless villains: With two large cross-cut saws, sawing into two feet lengths the planks which encased their victims, commencing at the feet of each, and then throwing the pieces into the unfinished Bungalow, set fire to it, and made off at the top of their speed along the high road towards Islempoora, a small village at no great distance, which had been appointed as a rendezvous for the whole to assemble at, when their bloody work at Goolampore had terminated.

Major Huntingdon had, early that morning, received private information of the intended outbreak, and the general plan of the mutineers. He was therefore prepared for the emergency, and acted accordingly; so that when the party of horse, accompanied by the Goolandowz (native artillery) arrived at the artillery lines, they found that the birds had flown; the gun sheds were empty, and those whom they thought to have found quietly taking their breakfasts, were, doubtless, then hovering around, ready to fire upon them at the first convenient opportunity; nor was there any one on whom they could wreak their vengeance, for the whole of the families of the Europeans had, by the prudence and determined conduct of their commanding officer, been removed to a place of safety within the walls of the Fort, where, but for the obstinacy and infatuation of General D——, the whole of the Europeans, unable to bear arms, might have found a refuge ere it was too late. Foiled in their attempt to capture the guns, without which they knew they could not hold possession of the town, they turned in the direction of the Bazaar, which they determined to plunder, then make their way to Islempoora. They shortly fell in with the Sepoy battalions, which had made the ineffectual attempt to carry the Fort by assault. Chafing with rage at their disappointment, they accompanied the cavalry, vowing vengeance on all the whites or other Christians that should fall into their hands. But their villainous designs were frustrated, for on the head of the column of cavalry, wheeling into the narrow road leading to the principal Bazaar, they beheld, much to their consternation, four of the guns of the horse artillery, which immediately opened upon them with grape and canister, which told fearfully among them, as the number of riderless and wounded horses plainly showed, and the irregular horse, not being trained to act in concert with the regular troops, the whole were thrown into confusion, and were unable to reform or advance upon the guns. By a rapid movement, Major Huntingdon had brought his two twelve pound Howitzers to play on the Sepoy battalion, with shrapnel, shell and spherical case, with considerable effect. The native officer who commanded them deployed his right wing into line, and sent the left to endeavour to take the artillery in flank or rear. But in order to accomplish this they had to make a *detour* to the right, and in so doing came to grief. The road they had taken led them across the open plain and in front of the station gun, a long thirty-two pounder. This movement had been anticipated by the artillery officer, consequently it was loaded with as much canister as was considered safe, and a Sergeant, who volunteered, was appointed to take charge, and act as circumstances might require. A small pit had been dug, in which the Sergeant was snugly ensconced, and there was nothing to indicate to those passing within a short distance, that there was anything to be feared from that quarter; but in this they were terribly mistaken, for at the right moment the gun belched forth its storm of bullets into the very centre of the little column of infantry with fearful effect. So unexpected was the charge that the utmost confusion prevailed, which was considerably increased by the sudden appearance of about one hundred well mounted horsemen, acting as cavalry, sweeping down upon them, sabreing right and left. This party of horsemen consisted of officers of all corps in garrison, and every other available European that could sit on a horse or handle a sabre, and had been quietly organized, in expectation of an event like the present, by Major Collingwood.

Repulsed at all points, the mutineers retreated as fast as possible. Their infantry, in many cases, mounting in rear of the cavalry. The artillery limbered up and followed them to the outskirts of the town, where, as they crossed the deep Nulla leading to the Islempoora road, the gallant Huntingdon again blazed away at them, reducing their numbers to a considerable extent; but it was not considered advisable to follow them any farther. The troop was then divided and the guns sent in different directions through the station, while the lately improvised cavalry scoured the Bazaars and other parts, in order to capture any small parties who might be engaged in the work of plunder or other destruction.

# CHAPTER XI.

The hour of eleven was ringing from the gurries or gongs at the different guard rooms, as Arthur Carlton left the quarters of the Brigadier commanding the station, for unlike most A.D.C.'s he did not reside with his chief, but occupied snug little quarters in the staff lines near the Suddur Bazaar. He was both annoyed and excited as he mounted his horse to return home; but he soon became calm and thoughtful, and his noble charger, as if knowing the mood of his master, slackened its speed to a walk. "General D—— is an obstinate and self-willed man, and his policy anything but what it should be at so critical a time," muttered Arthur half aloud; "but was I wise to cross him, and in the heat of the moment to throw up my appointment on his staff; I who have nothing but my pay to depend on and no interest at the Horse Guards to push me on in the service?" and his thoughts flew back to Vellenaux, Sir Jasper Coleman and Edith Effingham. As her image crossed his mind his countenance brightened, and his spirits rose. "Yes, I will rejoin my regiment. She must return to Rutlaum in a day or two. I will see her tomorrow and beg her to allow me to be her escort, that I think she will not refuse; and when I get my troop I will seek her hand, for her heart I know is mine already." He was aroused from his reverie by the sudden stopping of his horse, and on looking up found that he had arrived at the gate of the Compound which surrounded his dwelling. Immediately on entering he summoned his butler, and gave him instructions to pack up everything without delay, and to start with his baggage and the other servants at an early hour on the following morning, *en route* for Rutlaum; to halt at the first Dawk Bungalow he came to, and that he would follow on horseback in the evening. Then calling Pedro, a Portuguese, who had entered his service on his first arrival in India as a Kitmagar or Valet, he dispatched him to the Bazaar to procure from the Kotwell the necessary hackarries, or baggage carts and cattle; then, after enjoying several puffs from his hookah, he flung himself on a lounge to snatch what sleep he could before the grey dawn of day appeared. He was aroused at an early hour by the hurried entrance of his Portuguese servant who, after carefully closing the door, communicated the following startling intelligence: It appears that Pedro, after executing the commission entrusted to him, called on a friend in the Bazaar, who, like himself, was a Christian, to bid him farewell, and remained for two or three hours; that on his way home he heard voices in the angle of a small compound, which excited his curiosity. Approaching the spot noiselessly, through a hole in the prickly pear hedge he, by the light of the moon, saw four persons conversing together, two of whom he recognized; one was a Jemidar of Cavalry, the other, Soobadah, Major of one of the native regiments, the remaining two were strangers, evidently belonging to some irregular corps. The substance of their conversation was to the effect that, about six hundred irregular horse, and a company of Goolandowz, (but without guns or ammunition) were halted a short distance beyond the limits of the cantonments ready to enter at a given signal; that all the native corps in garrison were to rise, simultaneously, about eight a.m.; an attempt was to be made to carry off the artillery guns while the European gunners were at their breakfasts; the Fort was to be carried by a sudden rush, and the town plundered; they were then to make off to the next smallest station, where they were unlikely to meet with any European force.

For some moments Arthur was undecided as to what course he ought to pursue. "If," thought he, "I carry this information to the Brigadier, he will pooh, pooh it as mere moonshine, besides I no longer belong to his staff, and he would not listen to anything I might suggest; it would only be time thrown away; but Huntingdon must be warned. Forewarned is forearmed, and he is not the man to disregard a circumstance of this kind." He at once wrote a note relating what had been told him, and sent it by the Portuguese.

"You will deliver this into the hand of Major Huntingdon, and likewise give him a full account of all you saw and heard, and return as quickly as possible." The servant was soon on his way to the artillery lines. The next thing was to start his servants' baggage and personal effects by a road, directly opposite the one where the irregulars were said to be halted. While dressing and arming, he resolved as to what step he should now take. He would ride over to Edith, and, after placing her in safety within the walls of the Fort, join the other officers of the garrison under the direction of Major Collingwood and act as he deemed best in the coming struggle. He was well mounted and thoroughly armed, and likewise carried a double-barreled tiger-rifle, slung carbine-fashion to his saddle, and was as formidable a cavalier as one could meet with in the country. Giving his last instructions to Pedro, who, by this time, had returned, he rode out of the compound and took his way to the Bungalow, where all that he held most dear in life was, perhaps, sleeping, all unconscious of the impending danger. When he was near the house, a few shots were fired, and a hubbub was heard within the Sepoy lines.

"I am almost too late," thought Arthur, as he dashed up to the door. Edith, who had seen his approach met him in the verandah. A few words sufficed to explain how matters stood, and she hurried away to put on her riding habit, and gather together what valuables belonged to her. Arthur lost no time in causing to be saddled one of the best horses in the stable, and had it led round to the front of the Bungalow, where, in a very short time, he was joined by Edith, fully equipped for any emergency.

Placing her quickly and firmly on her saddle, and carefully examining every strap and buckle, and finding everything secure, he sprang lightly on his own steed. One glance at the space in front of the Bungalow, was quite sufficient to realize, to a practical mind like Arthur's, the imminent dangers that would beset them, should they attempt to cross the open plain in the direction of the Fort. The only chance was in a rapid flight. There was no time to arrange any definite plan of action, for a very few minutes would elapse before the mutineers would surround the Bungalow, and cut off all means of escape; so passing directly to the rear of the compound, they sought the cover of the jungle that skirted it. Advancing as rapidly as the narrow path and thickly interwoven underbrush would admit of, they soon left the station far behind them. At the foot of an eminence they emerged from the cover of the woods, and struck into the highroad that wound round the hill in front of them. This they ascended at a gentle canter, for Arthur was too good a rider to push his horses at the commencement of a journey, in which both speed and endurance might be required before its termination. His intention was, if possible, to reach Rutlaum; should he fail in this he must reach some station on the sea coast before night-fall, and place Edith under the protection of the officer commanding such post, until he could arrange for a passage for her to Bombay. On arriving at the crest of the hill, they turned to take a parting look at the pretty little station, where, for so many weeks, they had been supremely happy in the enjoyment of each others society, and framing projects for their union, at some future period, when the young Lieutenant should have advanced sufficiently in his profession to warrant that consummation so devoutly to be wished for.

Lurid flames and thick dark smoke shot up from many a burning Bungalow, while the roar of Artillery and discharge of musketry, convinced the fugitives that the conflict was still going on between the defenders of the Fort and the miscreants who vainly endeavoured to effect an entrance in order to put to death any Europeans who had taken shelter within its walls. Parties of Sepoys were looting the Bazaars and residences of the European officers of whatever they could lay their hands upon, while the cavalry, both regular and irregular, were riding hither and thither in search of Christian men, women, or children, who might have been unfortunate enough not to have gained admission to the Fort, or make good their escape from the fated place ere it was too late.

"Look, dearest Arthur," exclaimed Edith, pointing with her riding whip to a bend in the road some distance below them, "what are those horsemen? are they friends or foes? Oh! I see you change colour, and we are lost. But is there no hope for us?"

For a few moments Carlton remained silent, measuring with a practised eye the distance between those advancing and the spot on which they stood. For himself he had not a single thought, but for her in whom his whole soul was bound, the thought of what would be her fate, should she fall into the hands of those who he well knew were bent on their capture, it was this agonizing thought that caused a convulsive shudder to run through his whole frame, and rendered him for the moment speechless. But it was only for a moment; his deep love for the beautiful being at his side, and her imminent peril, roused him to immediate action.

"It would be wrong for me to attempt to conceal the fact of the great danger in which we stand. Our pursuers are irregular troops; men who have been taught to hate everything Christian, being the followers of petty Rajahs, who for some act of their own, or some of their families' treachery or disloyalty to our Government, lost their landed possessions, and consequently their revenue and power; but, dearest, they shall only reach you over my dead body. They would, in the long run, overtake us; but could we reach a wooden bridge that crosses a small river, a few miles up the road, I believe we could yet elude them. For there is an old road leading from the ford and running parallel with the one we are on. It has not been used for the past two years, and they, being strangers in this part of the country, will, in all probability, know nothing of it, and by this way we may escape. Courage, dearest Edith, all may yet go well with us."

"Your love and devotion, dear Arthur, I have never for one moment doubted, and confidently trust myself to your protecting arm and loving heart. But what can one single arm do against numbers; but should those wretches overtake us, the spirit of the Effinghams will teach me how to act, and, if necessary, how to die." As she said this, she drew from the folds of her riding habit, a handsome five-chambered revolver. "I will never become their prey, nor shall you perish unavenged while I have strength to draw a trigger," exclaimed the beautiful girl, now excited beyond measure at the critical position in which she found herself placed. "Brave and noble girl," responded Arthur, as he bent over and imprinted a kiss on the lovely brow. And in another moment they were bounding along the high road at a hand gallop.

"We are gaining on them," shouted one of the pursuers, as he caught sight of the two lovers flying along a straight piece of road at no very great distance in front of them. "But we shall have some tough work before we capture the young fellow or I am much mistaken."

"Curse him," growled out a tall athletic fellow in the uniform of a Russeldah. "I may thank him for my court martial and loss of commission in the regulars; but my turn is coming now. He and his dainty lady shall curse the hour of their birth before I have done with them. 'Remember,' said he, turning to the party, of whom he was evidently the leader, 'they must, if possible, be taken alive. Their money and valuables—and, doubtless, they have a good store about them—you can divide among yourselves; I will not touch one rupee of it; but their lives are mine." A shout of approval followed this last speech, and the whole party pushed forward with increased speed.

The little wooden bridge, referred to by Carlton, was at length gained. During the ride he had communicated to Edith the steps he intended to take on gaining the cover of the old road. Turning sharply to the right they entered the jungle, and made their way into the stream that crossed the road, then passing up the centre and under the bridge, they landed about one hundred and fifty paces higher up on the opposite bank, and, having dismounted, Arthur sought for, and soon found, the entrance to the road they were in search of, now overhung with brambles and creeping plants. Pushing them carefully aside, they entered, and found themselves in a narrow track, overgrown with soft grass. Assisting Edith to remount, Carlton threw the bridle of his own horse over the stump of a tree, then said to her, in a voice hoarse with emotion, and pointing to a small opening between the bushes, "From this point you can watch the results of my endeavours for our mutual safety. Should I fall, turn and fly. This road will lead you to Rutlaum." Then snatching a hasty kiss, he retraced his steps to the edge of the main road, taking up his position under the cover of the thick bushes.

The road leading to the bridge was, for about one hundred yards, perfectly straight, and much narrower than at other points, and the jungle at both sides was both thick and dense. Rather an awkward place for cavalry, should there be any infantry lurking in ambush, watching to give them a hot reception. I have said that Arthur was thoroughly armed; besides his two revolvers and sabre, he had his double-barreled tiger-rifle, a breech-loader of the newest pattern, which had only lately been introduced into India. Arthur had not long to wait for his foes, for the clattering of the armed hoofs of their troop horses were soon heard coming along at a rapid pace. There were nine of them, riding three abreast. As soon as they were within range, Carlton coolly levelled his rifle and discharged both barrels in rapid succession, shooting the centre file through the chest, who fell dead instantly, and lodging his other bullet in the shoulders of the horse of the file on his right, bringing both steed and rider to the ground, the latter underneath, his leg being crushed by the fall. So sudden and unexpected was the attack, that the two men who were riding immediately in rear, unable to check their speed in time, their horses stumbled and both their riders were thrown. They were, however, not much hurt by their fall and were soon in their saddles again. The dead and wounded men were removed to some soft grass on the side of the road. But this delay, short as it was, enabled Arthur to reload and shift his position, which he did by rapidly passing under the bridge to the opposite side of the road, being too good a soldier to neglect this opportunity.

"Forward!" shouted the Russeldah. "Follow me! I will soon unkennel the foe. May the grave of his fathers be accursed, and his bones be burned," and, after uttering this anathema, he drove the rowels of his spurs into his horse's flanks, springing him, at least, two lengths in advance of his followers, and making a dash for the bush from whence the smoke of the rifle was seen to issue. But ere the scoundrel reached it, a bullet from Arthur's rifle went crashing through his brain. A second brought another to the earth with a broken thigh bone. The others reined up in time to avoid the accident they had before experienced. On finding their leader to be quite dead, and only five of their number fit to carry on the contest, they consulted together as to the expediency of any further pursuit; besides, they could not understand being attacked from both sides of the road. They had seen no one cross, and never dreamed of the passage under the bridge, and imagined there must be others concealed in the jungle. Taking advantage of this opportunity, Arthur returned the way he came as quickly as possible, and, mounting his horse, regained his beloved Edith, who had witnessed the whole affair. She was about to thank, with ardent words of gratitude, her gallant lover, when he silenced her with a motion of his hand, and whispered to her to follow him. They proceeded slowly for a time, carefully avoiding the overhanging branches, lest they should attract the attention of either of the troopers, who were still halted on the high road at no great distance, and as Carlton afterwards affirmed, a chance shot from one of their carbines might have proved fatal to one or perhaps both of them. After riding some distance they had the satisfaction, on looking back, of seeing that their cowardly pursuers were returning the way they came, carrying their dead and wounded with them. But still they had a very long ride before them, under a scorching sun, before they could consider themselves safe from further pursuit; and the deep shadows of the dark jungle had closed around them as they pushed their way along the dusty road. And it was not until the moon had risen in all her splendour, high above their heads, that Edith, worn out with the excitement and fatigue of the day's journey, attended by a gallant cavalier, reached Rutlaum.

Fortunately, they experienced no difficulty in tracing the whereabouts of the Bartons, who had not, as yet, left the place. The news of the disaster at Goolampore had not reached Rutlaum, the mutineers having cut the telegraph lines, and the intelligence would not, in all probability, be received for a couple of days; and it was agreed that it should be suppressed as long as possible. It was arranged that the family should leave on the following evening by the Palkee Dawk for the coast. Carlton, of course, called on the officer commanding the post, and explained to him all he knew concerning the outbreak, and exactly how things stood when he left the station.

The Bartons were delighted to have Edith with them again, for nothing had gone right during her absence. Mrs. Barton had not been accustomed to take any part in the household arrangements or keeping the servants in order, consequently everything had gone wrong.

Edith grew eloquent when describing the dauntless courage of Carlton in rescuing her from a fate too horrible to be thought of. On hearing this, Arthur rose at least fifty per cent. in the estimation of Mrs. Barton, with whom he had always been a great favourite, and she warmly thanked him for the exertion he had made in behalf of her young friend. Taking advantage of the opportunity thus afforded him, Arthur, on the spur of the moment, disclosed to her everything concerning his engagement to Edith, and solicited their approval to the union on his attaining the rank of Captain. He was warmly supported by Edith, who did not hesitate to declare her affection for one whom she had known so long, and who had risked so much for her. And when Mrs. Barton found that the wedding was not to take place for some time, and that Edith was to return with them to England, she professed herself to be satisfied on the subject, whereupon it was arranged that the party should proceed to the sea coast. On reaching Doollia, the lovers parted in hopes of meeting again at no distant day in England, for the ratification of those vows that were exchanged during their ride for life through the Goozeratte.

Independent of the inward satisfaction felt by Edith, that her engagement to Arthur had met the approval of the kind friends to whom she owed so much, she experienced a great deal of pleasure during the overland journey to Europe. Both Horace and Pauline had twice traversed the route, and therefore were enabled to point out the various objects of interest that were met with in the different places they passed through. The Egyptian Pyramids, Cleopatra's Needle, and the far-famed Catacombs at Alexandria, with many a new and strange sight, encountered during their short sojourn at Malta and Gibraltar, which had been unheeded on her passage out, so depressed and sad at heart had she felt at the death of her uncle. But, time having healed that mental wound, and a bright future opening before her, she could now fully enjoy those scenes and the associations they usually call up.

# CHAPTER XII.

Arthur Carlton lost no time in making his way to the Capital and reporting himself to the Commander-in-Chief. His Excellency was pleased to accept graciously his reasons for throwing up his appointment on the staff of General D――, at Goolampore. Our hero had expected to get a good rap over the knuckles for acting as he had done without first applying to headquarters, and this, doubtless, would have been the case at any other time, but the blind folly and general mismanagement of the late Brigadier had already been commented upon and censured by the authorities, and no doubt if death had not interfered to prevent it, a court martial and dismissal from the service would have been the result. As it was, another officer was sent up and appointed to the command at Goolampore, and Lieutenant Carlton ordered to join his regiment at the earliest opportunity, which, of course, meant that he should proceed with any corps, detachment, or party that might be moving in that direction. But Arthur was too anxious for active employment to brook any such delay; so, after a few days' sojourn at the Capital, attended only by his servants, took the road to Runjetpoora, where his regiment was reported to be stationed. Nothing, of interest occurred on the route, until within a few miles of his destination where he expected to join his corps.

It being his last day's march, he had sent his servants and baggage on several hours in advance, and being well armed and well mounted, he started from his halting place about daylight, alone, and pursued his course along the high road, in the best possible spirits, feeling well contented with the position of things in general, and his own in particular.

About noon, being somewhat heated and thirsty, he turned his horse's head to the right, and rode quietly some distance into the jungle, and finding a cool shady spot by a small running stream, dismounted, and taking off the saddle from his charger, gave him a feed of gram or corn, and allowed a sufficient length of tether to enable him to crop the soft grass which grew in the immediate vicinity of the running stream just alluded to, while he rested and regaled himself with some biscuits, brandy punnee, and his favourite German pipe. He had taken up his position at the foot of a small tree, with his back against the trunk, his famous tiger-rifle lying by his side and the hilt of his sabre within convenient handling distance, for the time and place was such that these precautions could not, with safety, be neglected. While thus resting, he sank into a deep reverie; his thoughts wandering back to his school boy days, in merry old England, ere he had sighed for a sword and feather or longed to seek the bubble reputation at the cannon's mouth, or dreamed of scenes by flood and field, beneath the scorching suns, over the arid plains, or amid the wild trackless jungles of Industan.

Then Vellenaux, the home of his happy youth with its architectural grandeurs, its magnificent parks and rich woodland scenery, passed in review like a panorama before his mental vision, but fair as these visions were, another far brighter rose before which all others paled or faded by comparison. Edith, in all her glorious beauty, now riveted his every thought, engrossed the whole stretch of his imagination, and for the time rendered all else opaque and obscure; for had she not promised to become his wife, to share with him the varied fortunes of a soldiers' life, to be the joy and solace of his riper years, and heart in heart and hand in hand, to glide together, as it were, almost imperceptibly into the yellow leaf of ripe old age. Again, like the ever varying pictures of light and shade, his thoughts turned on the present,—this campaign over, the mutiny crushed out, and the command of a troop conferred upon him, he would be in a position to return to England, claim his bride, and thus would the dearest wishes of his heart be fully realized. From this delightful train of thought, he was aroused by the cracking and breaking of the dry leaves and brush wood at some little distance, yet immediately in front of him, and ere he had time to rise, an enormous tiger, a regular Bengalle, sprang over the intervening bushes on the open space, within a few yards of where Carlton was quietly smoking. This sudden appearance was as unlooked for by our hero as was Carlton's figure by the royal beast himself, and, for a few seconds, they gazed on each other. But Arthur's presence of mind on such occasions never deserted him. Instantly bringing to his shoulder the rifle that lay handy by his side, and without moving his position, he covered and took deliberate aim at his—to say the least of it—just then unwelcome visitor. Until the cocking of the rifle, the enormous brute seemed undecided as to what course to pursue. But no sooner did this sound reach the tiger, than his long tail began to sway slowly backwards and forwards two or three times; and, with a low growl, fierce and deep, settled himself gradually back on his haunches, preparatory to making that spring which this class of animals are so famous for, and which in many instances prove so fatal to those who pursue or oppose them. But Arthur was a cool and energetic hunter, and had scoured the jungles for weeks together, and had brought in more trophies of his skill, as a Shirkarree, than any other man in the regiment, and ere the spring could be completed, for the animal had risen in the air, Arthur had planted a brace of bullets in the chest of the monster, literally cracking, in their progress, the heart of the tiger, who fell forward stone dead within six feet of where our hero was seated. His practical eye in an instant convinced him that no danger was to be apprehended from his late foe, and without changing his attitude, resumed the pipe, he had let fall from his lips prior to firing, and, as unconcerned as though nothing of moment had taken place, commenced carefully to reload his rifle. While thus engaged, the crushing among the branches of the jungle trees, and the cracking of the withered stocks and leaves again attracted his attention; and presently some half dozen horsemen cleared the adjacent bushes and reined up suddenly on the brink of the little brook before alluded to, with surprise and astonishment depicted on their glowing and excited features, as they gazed on the scene, thus unexpectedly presented to their view.

"By Jove! did I not know that Arthur Carlton was hundreds of miles away up in the North-West, I could swear that was he," pointing to the figure of Carlton seated at the foot of the tree, exclaimed the foremost rider, as he with difficulty curbed in his impatient steed.

"And who else but the Burra Shirkarree, the Carlton Sahib, would you expect to find within a couple of yards of the carcass of a lord of the jungle, just slaughtered by him, and cooly re-loading as if he had only been shooting at a pidgeon match," said Travas Templeton in reply, dismounting as he spoke, and advancing quickly, seized and shook warmly the hand of our hero, who had by this time sprang to his feet.

"You guessed right this time, Travas, old fellow," said Carlton, giving his friend another hearty shake of the hand. Then, turning to the first speaker, whom he addressed as Dorville, said, "So you thought me miles away, did you? I was sure you had seen the General's order for me to rejoin. Pray, introduce me to your friends, and we can have a mutual explanation of how we came to meet thus unexpectedly." This being done, the whole party dismounted and threw themselves at full length within such shade as the jungle afforded, and listened to Arthur's account of the outbreak at Goolampore, and his reasons for throwing up his appointment on the staff; the unexpected appearance of the tiger and the death of the same.

"A ticklish thing to do, by Jove, to take the matter in your own hands in that fashion. But all's well that ends well, and devilish glad will our fellows be to learn that you will be so soon among us again, especially as your troop and mine have been ordered out on some special service, and that accounts for our presence in this neighborhood, and so far from headquarters; but Travas will give you the particulars;" and lighting a cheroot, Francis Dorville puffed out numberless circles of pale, blue smoke, which he appeared to enjoy with infinite satisfaction.

"Then you must know, most redoubtable of tiger-slayers," began Travas Templeton, who was a cornet in Arthur's troop, and an enthusiastic sportsman, "that the Brigadier commanding, having secretly got wind that a party of mutineers had ensconced themselves in a small fortress, among yonder hills," pointing with his cigar in the direction as he spoke, "has ordered a flying column, of which two troops of ours form a part, to attack, and, if possible, to carry the place by assault or *coup de main*; that we are encamped about eight miles to the South-West of this spot. Last night some villagers came in and reported that a large tiger, doubtless the identical one yonder, was causing great havoc among the cattle; so some half dozen of us started this morning in pursuit. We caught sight of the brute about a mile from here, and Dorville, being green at this kind of sport, took a shot at him at too great a range, and, of course, missed, sending the creature in your direction, and so gave you the opportunity of bagging him, which you have most successfully accomplished."

"I am sorry, gentlemen, to have deprived you of your day's sport, but under the circumstances, I really could not have done anything less, for the tiger came so suddenly upon me, that there was nothing else for it; but this really will be capital fun, the expedition to the hill fort you speak of," replied Arthur as he tossed off the remaining portion of his brandy punnee, exclaiming at same time, "Here's all success to our new undertaking."

"You will give up all idea, of course, of going on to Runjetpoora, and return with us to our camp and join our troop, for we are to attack these gentry to-morrow evening, I believe. Colonel Atherly, of the engineers, commands the column. He has heard of your exploits at Mooltan and Chillianwalla, and would be sorry to lose the services of so good a Sabre on this occasion. You can report in writing to headquarters, through his Deputy-Adjutant-General, that you have joined your troop. Your tent and servants can be sent over to you during to-morrow; in the meantime, you can share mine,"—"or mine,"—"or mine,"—shouted a chorus of voices.

"Upon my word, Dorville, you are highly complimentary. It's very flattering to a fellow's feelings to be so thoroughly appreciated, especially, after so long an absence from the regiment. Devilish kind of you, gentlemen, to offer me quarters among you; but, as I cannot divide myself into half a dozen pieces, I shall only be too happy to accept our friend Dorville's offer, he being first in the field. By George, it will be rejoining with *eclat* if that little fort up yonder, on the hill side, could be carried by one bold dash, and the affair terminated in a day or so," cried Carlton, his handsome face lighting up, and pleasure beaming from his flashing eye at the bare idea of the coming contest.

"If I can only get my twenty-four pound howitzer in a good position I will make the place so hot in a dozen hours that the blackguards will curse their unlucky stars that caused them to unlimber for action in such an owl's nest as that," put in another of the party, an artillery officer, attached to the flying column.

"But what say you to a move, gentlemen. We have some miles to ride, and that, too, before the trumpet sounds the mess call," said Travas, raising himself from his sitting position and moving towards his horse. This suited the views of the whole party. The greater number were already in the saddle. While Arthur and the two others had their feet in the stirrup, preparing to mount, the whole party were startled and amazed by the very novel and unlooked for apparition of a female figure, flying towards them, evidently in great terror and alarm. On reaching Carlton, who was the nearest to her, she bent forward with supplicating looks and clasped hands, passionately exclaiming, "Oh! for pity sake, hasten to the rescue, ere it be too late. Fly! gentlemen, and stay the bloody work of those miscreants, those fiends in human form. Oh! waste not a moment, or your aid may come too late." The supplicant was a handsome three-quarter cast. Her luxuriant hair, dark as a raven's wing, hung in wild confusion about her neck and shoulders. Her well-fitting dress, of fine Madras muslin, hung in shreds around her finely moulded form, and blood was issuing from rents in her light kid slippers, caused, doubtless, by the thorns and other prickly obstacles she had met with on her passage through the tangled brushwood of the jungle.

"Pray, calm yourself, I beg, and endeavour to collect your thoughts. To whom do you allude, and in what direction; do you wish us to go?" said Dorville, as he handed her some sherry and water from his flask; this she drank eagerly, then hurriedly continued—the whole group pressing nearer and nearer to the excited woman, to learn by what mischance or accident she had been thrown amongst them at such a time and place, so suddenly—"The Collector of Runjetpoora, his wife, daughter, and sister, with his four clerks, their wives and children, have been attacked and captured by a band of twenty mounted mutineers, who have sworn to massacre them, and some of the children have already been cruelly butchered by these remorseless villains; I, alone, escaped, and sought shelter in the jungle, where, from an opening down the ravine, caught a glimpse of your party, and have struggled through brake and briar to implore your assistance. Oh! do not lose a moment, if you would be in time. Even now it may be too late to save them;" and, weeping wildly, sank on her knees, convulsive sobs choking her further utterance.

There was now no need to urge them on, for they at once realized the horrors of the position in which the Collector and his party were now placed. Exclamations of anger, and vows of bitter vengeance burst from the lips of all, as they, with paling cheek, and flashing eye, their teeth clenched fiercely together, listened to the appaling tale of the half frantic girl before them.

"They are but three to one, the pack of mutinous scoundrels, and cannot resist our charge five minutes, and must go down before well-tried sabres," cried Carlton, springing into his saddle, and taking the lead, saying, as he did so, "Point out the way we should take, my good girl, and what courage, brave hearts, and trusty swords can effect, shall be done to rescue your friends from the terrible fate which, doubtless, awaits them."

"When you reach that single tree on the crest of yonder hill," indicating with her right hand the direction to be taken, "you will come in sight of the place, where this villainous outrage has been committed; your own judgment will then tell you what is best to be done," she replied, evidently strengthened and refreshed by the wine she had taken, and the comforting assurance held out to her by Arthur and his companions. These words had scarcely passed her lips when, applying the spur vigorously, the whole party, with one exception, dashed off in the direction indicated. Captain Crosby of the artillery, who had not started with the rest, feeling somewhat anxious for the poor girl's safety—alone as she would be shortly in that dense jungle, for every Sabre would be needed in the coming onslaught—approaching her, said kindly and gently, "and you; what is to become of you? what will you do, or where can you go?" "Oh, do not think of me," she replied, "I can retrace my steps the way I came, alone and unassisted," moving a few steps in that direction. "But stay one moment," said Crosby; "take this it may assist you in clearing a pathway through the thicket and underbrush," handing her, as he spoke, his long hunting knife. Raising her beautiful eyes to his, with a look of thankfulness, she accepted the weapon. In another instant, the ringing of horses' hoofs, now growing fainter in the distance, told her that help was hastening on to where help was most required.

# CHAPTER XIII.

The spot where the Collector and his party had been surprised and captured, was on the high road, midway between the Khandish Ghaut and the large and populous town of Runjetpoora, the inhabitants of which, with the exception of their Begum, or Princess, and a few of her immediate followers, had thus far remained faithful to British rule, and to which place he was now returning, after making a tour of inspection through the districts, which inspection consisted in surveying and valuing the crops while growing, the cattle and other properties of those residing within his jurisdiction, so that taxes might be levied on each individual according to their wealth and substance, during the current year.

The baggage escort and principal servants had been sent on in advance. This the mutineers were, doubtless, aware of, or counted on as being likely to be the case, therefore little opposition was to be expected, and so suddenly did they sweep down upon them that the little party were surrounded and overpowered ere they could seize their weapons to defend themselves. All were made prisoners save one, Mrs. de Mello, a handsome three-quarter caste, the youthful bride of the Collector's clerk or first assistant, who had alighted from her palkee to gather some wild flowers that grew on the road side, a short time prior to the appearance of the mutineers, and from where she stood witnessed the attack. Terrified beyond measure at her dangerous proximity to the ruffians, she fled for safety into the depths of the jungle, and so escaped.

The carriage and bullock games were drawn to an open space some little distance into the jungle, the intervening bushes screening it to a considerable extent from the road. The Collector and his clerks were then brutally stripped of their clothing, and, having taken possession of their money and other valuables, the wretches bound them, spread eagle fashion, to the wheels of the vehicles. The terrified women were next dragged forth, with more indignity and even greater brutality, and secured in a similar manner, and in such a position that their tortures might be witnessed by their helpless husbands. The children, with the exception of the Collector's daughter, a bright, golden haired girl of some ten summers, who had clung convulsively to her mother, were thrown together into a small hollow in the ground about the centre of the place, they being too young to make any opposition, the black devils forming a complete semi-circle round their intended victims.

The first scene of the bloody drama they proposed to enact, to satisfy their devilish thirst for the blood of the unfortunates, who had thus fallen into their hands, was opened by a tall, burly ruffian bending over, seizing one of the children, hurling it into the air, and yelling with an awful imprecation while so doing, that he would wager a gold mohur to five rupees, that he could, with his tulwa, strike off the child's right arm at the elbow without touching any other part of the body. This was accepted at once by half-a-dozen voices; the wretch immediately raised his tulwa and, as the infant descended, made a sharp, quick, upper cut, and ere it reached the ground its little arm was disjointed, as though by the knife of an experienced surgeon. A groan of horror burst from the lips of the agonized parents, and a convulsive shudder ran through the remainder of the unhappy party; but this past unheeded by their captors, being drowned by the yells of fiendish delight and approval that broke forth from the throats of these hell hounds, as the mutilated body of the child lay wreathing in agony at their feet, absorbing for the moment all other feeling. "I will double the stakes," cried another, "that I take off the head of a second of these young imps close to the shoulder without making wound or scar on any other part." "Done, and done again!" shouted several voices, throwing up their weapons in the air, and re-catching them again, so delighted were they at the idea of another spectacle so much in unison with their blood-thirsty and relentless passions. A powerful ruffian now dismounted, and catching up a second babe, a pretty little thing scarcely two years old, hurled it with his utmost strength high into the air. On gaining its greatest altitude, it turned completely, and was descending, head downwards. When within six feet of the ground, the brutal villain, with one lightning stroke of his tulwa, severed the head from its shoulders, amid the shouts and gesticulations of the assembled miscreants. By some, the wretch was pronounced a winner, but on examining the body, the skin of one shoulder was found to be grazed or cut. Many maintained it was done by the sword; others asserted that it was caused by falling on a stone or some such substance. The dispute ran high, and possible might have come to blows, but for the interference of another of the party, who appeared to be a sort of leader among them, shouting out "Come! No more of this fooling; too much time has been already wasted on this Tumahsha. Give the cursed feringees a volley from your carbines, loot the garries, and then make off with all speed, or the cursed Kaffirs may get wind of the affair and follow in our track."

"Shumsodeen is right," called out another. "There is both truth and reason in what he says. But there must be no firing, it might attract the notice of any straggler from the camps of those dogs of Kaffirs, and bring their infernal Dragoons down upon us. No! cut the throats of the men, and as there are but twenty of us, and only five of these women, tell off one of them to each four of us, and let us begone, for we must put the broad plain, at the foot of the Khandish Ghaut, between us and this place ere night fall, and on our camping for the night, each four can decide what is to be done with their prize." This suggestion was received with applause, and they immediately prepared to act upon it. Already two or three had dismounted and drawn their creeses to slit the throats of their male prisoners, when a youth, about eighteen, son of the fellow called Shumsodeen, cried out, "Do as you please with the women among yourselves, but I will have yonder curly headed cutcha butchee for my prize, come what may," and he took a few steps in the direction of the Collector's daughter, who was still clinging to her parent for protection; but ere he reached her, a loud, clear voice at no great distance rang out, "Fire! gentlemen, and charge!" Then came from between the leaves and bushes a withering volley of bullets from rifle and revolver, striking down the youth, and emptying three saddles, the riders falling lifeless to the ground. In another instant the branches parted, and Arthur Carlton, with his six companions, cleared the low brushwood, and sword in hand dashed into the centre of the ruffianly group.

Although taken completely by surprise—for they had not calculated upon being interfered with, especially at so early a period of their proceedings or by so formidable a foe—the mutineers instantly prepared to give their unexpected assailants a fierce and bloody reception. They fought frantically with a courage born of desperation, well knowing that to cut through their foes and escape by flight was their only chance; for should they not perish by the sword in the present contest, a halter, or to be blown to fragments from the cannon's mouth, would be their doom if made prisoners, consequently they rained down their blows frantically, and made several desperate attempts to break through or divide the small party that opposed them. But the cool and determined courage and thorough discipline of the Dragoons, and their friends was too much for them, fighting as they did, for a time, on the defensive; warding off the cuts of the dusky villains, and giving only a few thrusts here and there, when it could be done with fatal effect. Many of their number had already bit the dust, and, as yet, no impression had been made on the gallant little band, the Soaws being still two to one. Thus Carlton and his party were still fighting under a disadvantage as far as numbers were concerned. Had the combatants been less pre-occupied with their deadly strife, they might have observed, at a short distance, a female figure cautiously emerging from between the bushes and stealthily creep beneath the vehicle, to the wheels of which the Collector had been bound. This was the wife of the head clerk, the pretty three-quarter caste, whose presence of mind, courage and forethought had so largely contributed to their deliverance. Rapidly but surely, with the hunting knife given her by Captain Crosby, she cut the cords that bound her husband and his companions, who, when they found they were released, rushed forward and possessed themselves of the weapons of the fallen mutineers, and immediately commenced an attack on their flank and rear, in hopes of rendering some assistance to their brave defenders.

Moving quickly, but in such a way as not to attract notice, Mrs. de Mello, released the Collector's wife and the other ladies from their unpleasant and exposed position, and one by one removed them for safety within the cover of the jungle in case of any chance shot or blow injuring them. A brief time served to restore the ladies to something like tranquility, and enable them to arrange their attire to the best advantage under the circumstances, and evincing in the highest manner their thanks and gratitude to her who had, with such peril to herself, relieved them from a fate, to them, worse than death itself.

The unexpected release of the prisoners, and the attack made on their flank and rear by them, totally confounded the mutineers, and rendered all escape on their part impossible or nearly so, while Arthur and his friends, seeing the addition to their number, and being about equally matched—numerically speaking—changed their tactics from the defensive to the offensive, and attacked their opponents in right good earnest, and with such skill and determination did they use their weapons that they very shortly brought the contest to a close. Eleven of the mutinous rascals lay stone dead upon the blood-stained sod, and five others so fatally wounded that it would be impossible for them to survive another hour, three more were slightly injured, but sufficiently so to render them for the present *hors de combat*, while the one remaining wretch who had escaped scathless had sullenly thrown down his arms and stood looking on in moody silence. Every one of the brave little party that had come thus opportunely to the rescue, had been more or less injured by the Tulwas and pistol shots of the black Sowas, but in no case did their wounds render them unfit for active service; rest for a few days, together with some sticking plaster, was all that they needed to enable them to take the field again. Of the mutineers, the five mortally wounded were left to keep guard over the eleven dead, the remaining four were bound and lashed to one of the garries belonging to the Collector. The oaths and imprecations of these wretched beings at the failure of their project and the position they now found themselves in, were something fearful to listen to.

After a brief time, for congratulations, rest and refreshments, which refreshment consisted chiefly in brandy punnee, sherry and biscuit, from the flasks and wallets of the party, (no bad thing by the way, under the circumstance.) Matters then having been got *en train*, the whole party proceeded leisurely to the camp near Laurieghur, and arrived just as the sun was casting her golden rays on the slopes of the adjacent hills, previous to its sinking for the night into the purple depths of obscurity. Early the following morning, the Collector, with a suitable escort, proceeded on their way to Runjetpoora, the place to which they were returning when they were so ruthlessly set upon by the atrocious mutineers.

The day proceeding the one on which Arthur had joined his troop, the officer in command of the little force ordered a court martial to assemble for the trial of the prisoners concerned in the late murderous attack on the Collector and party. The finding of the court was, that the prisoners were guilty of all the charges brought against them, and the sentence pronounced was that of death, by being blown to fragments from the cannon's mouth, the sentence to be carried into effect the day succeeding the promulgation of the order for the execution. Preparations were then to be pushed forward vigorously for carrying by assault Laurieghur, the fortress among the hills. Already a heavy breaching battery had been sent for to Runjetpoora, for on a party of Engineers advancing more closely and with the aid of their field glasses, it was found to be a more formidable place, and more strongly guarded than had been anticipated by those in command at Runjetpoora; thus the delay in commencing the attack.

On the evening prior to the execution of the wretched criminals, as Arthur Carlton was quietly smoking a cigar and meditating on Edith, the approaching siege, and things in general, an orderly came to his tent and announced to him, that one of the prisoners desired to speak with him on a subject that admitted of no delay. Surprised at so unlooked for an event, Arthur at first felt inclined to refuse the man's request, but presently, curiosity getting the better of the dislike he felt at having any communication with the wretch, and wondering what he could possibly have to communicate, sent word that he would visit him soon after sun set.

"What is it you have to say to me?" enquired Arthur Carlton, an hour later, as with stern composure and folded arms, he looked down upon the wretched culprit who lay manacled on the floor of the guard tent, and who proved to be the youth before alluded to, as the son of the man called Shumsodeen.

The captive, with much difficulty raising himself to a sitting posture, said, "You are a brave man, and the brave among the whites are always truthful they tell me. I am told that I am to be blown from the cannon's mouth to-morrow. Is this the truth? Is there no hope of pardon or reprieve?"

"The sentence of the court has been read to you, and there is no hope of remission. You will die at sunrise to-morrow morning, and have but a few hours to live. This you might have ascertained from the sergeant of the guard without sending for me," said Arthur, turning to leave the tent.

"Stay!" resumed the prisoner, observing Carlton's intention, "I have that to say which nearly concerns yourself and companions. I have learned that it is the intention of your commander to carry the Fort of Laurieghur by assault; this cannot be done without great loss of life among you, for the place is much stronger and better provisioned and garrisoned than he has any idea of. Listen to my story, you will then see that I have it in my power to render your General a very great service if permitted to do so."

"Speak on," responded Arthur, getting somewhat interested, and seating himself on a bag of tent pegs, the the only apology for a seat the tent afforded.

The youth then proceeded with his story, from which it appeared that, about five weeks previous, a party of cavalry Sowas, regular and irregular, who had deserted their regiments, had arrived at the village in which the speaker and his father, who was a mounted police patell, resided. While there, the emissaries of the Begum of Runjetpoora, who had established herself at Laurieghur, and was organizing a force and getting together supplies of ammunition, provisions, etc., with the intention of making a raid on Runjetpoora and looting it, had made overtures to this party, and promised them high pay and a share of the plunder if they would join her. This they had accepted, and some of the men of the village, the father and son included, had cast in their lots with the mutineers and entered the fort; but, dissatisfied with being so long cooped up within its walk, and seeing no prospect of immediate plunder, had attempted to leave the place, but were prevented from so doing by the Begum's order. In sullen silence they received this injunction, but determined to escape when opportunity offered. That one day while he, (the prisoner) was passing through the ruins of a deserted palace, he had discovered the entrance to a subterraneous passage, leading under the walls and coming out about a quarter of a mile from the fort. This he had communicated to his comrades, and the following morning ere it was light, the party, led by himself, made good their retreat, and keeping within the jungle for some miles, came upon the high road, and chanced to meet the Collector's party; that he had taken no part in the slaughter of the children, and had intended leaving the band as soon as they came in sight of his own village, and in conclusion said, "If you will swear to obtain my pardon, and liberty to go where I please, I will lead you and any number of your men through this same passage, and in less than two hours from leaving this place, you shall be in possession of the fort and all it contains." This offer our hero did not consider himself at liberty to refuse or accept, but promised at once to bring the matter to the notice of the officer commanding the force, and let him (the prisoner) know the result as speedily as might be, and immediately left the guard room for that purpose.

The prisoner's proposition was at once accepted by the authorities, and very shortly a party of five hundred infantry, and one hundred dismounted dragoons, led by Carlton and accompanied by the prisoner as guide, left the camp and soon made their way without difficulty, or exciting the notice of the insurgents, through the subterraneous passage before alluded to into the fort, and the whole party were soon ensconced within the ruins of the old palace, without the garrison having the least idea of their presence in that quarter. On gaining this position, the signal agreed on, a blue light, was burned for one minute, then the whole force in camp turned out, and a demonstration was made from every available cannon and musket, as if the storming of the fort had commenced in earnest. The consternation of the mutineers at finding themselves so suddenly attacked was very great, and imagine their dismay on rushing to the walls, to find the ramparts lined with our men. Unable to account their appearance there, and believing treachery to be at work among themselves, and that the gates had been opened to admit the foe, threw down their arms and surrendered at discretion.

Search was immediately made for the Begum, and while looking for this mutiness Princess in one of her apartments, Carlton took up from a teapoy or dressing table, a small but curiously carved steel casket. Supposing it to contain cosmetics, or what was more probable, chinaum and beetle nut, hurriedly slipped it into his sabretache; but not succeeding in finding the Begum, who had evaded the pursuit, Arthur, with his Dragoons, returned to camp. The same evening the three villains already condemned were executed.

But the youth who had acted as guide was permitted to escape, which he lost no time in doing. The little force was then broken up, and the troop composing it sent back to their respective corps, while our hero and his Dragoons joined their regiment, and with it saw a great deal of hard fighting and rough service, and on more than one occasion his dashing conduct had been brought to the notice of the Indian Government.

The return of the troop from Persia, and the efficient manner in which the brigades under Sir Hugh Rose, Havelock, Mitchell, Whitlock and others were handled, proved too much for the mutineers, and after an obstinate contest which lasted over two years, during which time a heavy loss of life had been sustained on both sides, the rebellious native troops were beaten at all points, and law and order once more restored throughout the country.

# CHAPTER XIV.

Horace, on reaching London, had taken a house on Berkly Square. Old Mr. and Mrs. Barton having died some two years previous, as already stated, and the Willows in Devonshire had been let. He found his sister, Mrs. Ashburnham, still living on Cavendish Square, and Emily residing with her aunt in Harley street. Tom and his bride were still travelling on the Continent. Mr. and Mrs. Barton therefore determined to remain in town until the lease, for which the country seat had been let, should expire, which would take place about the month of August in the following year; and thus it was that the people of Vellenaux knew nothing of their return to England. Fond of gaiety and fashionable life, Mrs. Barton determined to make up for time lost during their sojourn in the Goozeratte, by being very gay, attending balls, parties and operas, and not unfrequently giving stylish entertainments at her house at Berkly Square, in all of which Edith participated, as her kind friend would go no where and do nothing without her, and thus she passed her first season in London. In the spring of the year she received the welcome intelligence that Arthur had been promoted to a troop, and that if he could manage to obtain leave of absence, he would be in England early in summer to claim his bride.

"Well, my dear," said Mrs. Barton, a few days subsequent to the receipt of the letter, "Horace, dear old fellow, has arranged everything nicely for you. He has still some interest with the authorities. He has been to the India office. Arthur is to have eighteen months leave of absence, and before the expiration of that time his regiment will be ordered home; so you see, my dear, we shall be able to see a great deal of each other. After you are married you will, of course, remain with us until it is time for Arthur to rejoin his regiment." Edith felt very grateful to her kind friends for all they had done to further her happiness, and looked forward to the time when she should meet her affianced husband with intense satisfaction and delight. She would not now be called upon to return to India, to which country she had a strong aversion; and well she might, for her residence there, with the exception of her episodes of pleasure derived from the society of Arthur, had indeed been very trying.

It was summer, bright, glorious, balmy summer. The birds sang and chirped among the green leaves, and wood pigeons cooed in the hollow trunks of the trees, beneath whose outspreading branches, little four-footed creatures gamboled and made merry among the soft feathery grasses that grew in the fine old beech woods of Devon. It was pleasant to listen to the cool, gurgling sound of the brawling brook, whose bright waters skipped, danced and glittered, as they forced their way over the pebbles and other impediments in their serpentine course along the shady dell that skirted the Home Park, wherein, under the venerable oaks, the red and fallow deer rested, dreamily sniffing the delicious fragrance that pervaded the air, borne upon the light summer wind from the rich parterre which stretched the entire length of the south wing at Vellenaux.

In a large octagon-shaped apartment that had been fitted up as a library, the most pleasing feature of which was its Southern aspect, were seated *tete a tete* two personages, who figured somewhat conspicuously in the early part of our story, these were Mrs. Fraudhurst and Sir Ralph Coleman. They had met here at the request of the Baronet, for Sir Ralph and the widow rarely met except by appointment or at the dinner table.

Time had dealt kindly with the lady, and what was deficient by nature was supplied by art, for she was one of those who always paid the most scrupulous attention to their toilette. If we were to describe her as fat, fair, and forty, we should certainly wrong her. Fair and forty she undoubtedly was, but fat she certainly was not. There was a slight tendency to embonpoint, but this was relieved by her tall and not ungraceful figure. She was what might be termed a decidedly handsome woman. The corpulent lawyer had subsided into the sleek, well-conditioned country gentleman. But there was at times a certain restlessness of the eye, and a nervous twitching at the corners of the mouth, which, to a keen observer, would indicate that he was not always the quiet, self-possessed person that he would have his neighbors to believe. The business on which they had met had been interrupted by the entrance of a servant with a note to Sir Ralph, but, on his leaving the room, the conversation was resumed by Mrs. Fraudhurst saying:

"I would much rather, Sir Ralph, that this subject be now discontinued, and never again reverted to. The papers to which you allude are perfectly safe in my hands, and I do not see that any good could accrue by my transferring them to you, certainly none to myself, and it might militate against me; for the great anxiety you evince to get possession of the documents leads me to believe that you have some particular object in view, something which does not appear or, the surface, and which you desire should not come to my knowledge."

"But, my dear madam, you surely do not imagine that I have any other motive in requesting you to hand over to my safe keeping the deed in question than a natural desire to be quite certain that our mutual interests should not be imperilled by any accidental circumstance that might disclose the existence of any such document."

The lady looked steadily at him for a few seconds, then in a clear distinct, and deliberate tone, said, "For the last seven years the will of the late Baronet has been in my possession, during which, time you, Sir Ralph, have made frequent attempts to obtain it from me, sometimes on one pretence, then on another. Were I to agree to your request, what security have I that you, who have acted so vile a part against Miss Effingham, would not act as treacherously towards me, were I once in your power? While I possess that document, I hold my position here, and can thus keep you at bay. And think you that I will thus surrender my advantage to please the idle fancy of a man who would not hesitate to stoop to perform any act however dastardly, so that he could effectually escape the penalty of a crime he was ready to profit by, but cowardly enough to shrink from the consequences it entailed? You say that our interest in this affair is mutual,—it is not so, and you know it. You gain nineteen thousand a year, I only one. Again, should the will by any mischance be found in my possession, who would believe my statement that you were a party concerned in the abstraction of the said deed, you would deny all knowledge of the transaction and my unsupported evidence could not commit you. Of course you would lose the estate; but what would my condition be then. No! I have everything at stake—you, comparatively nothing. I will not accede to so absurd a proposition." There was a short pause, the widow resumed her embroidery with an air of apparent indifference. The baronet sat abstractedly gazing out of the window, evidently turning over something in his mind. As she had stated he had tried to wheedle her out of the papers, but she had hitherto, by great tact, adroitly managed to shift the conversation to some other subject, in a quiet and playful manner. He was therefore not prepared for this vehement outburst; she had not only refused to comply with his demand, but taunted him with stinging words for his pusillanimous conduct. He knew her great ambition, and that the sole object of her life was to become mistress of Vellenaux, and to gain this she would risk everything. It was her weak point, the only vulnerable part he could attack with any hope of success. He had for months pondered over this; it had this advantage, it is true, he thought a marriage would secure him in the possession of both the will and her silence; but then he hated her with a cordial hate. He had been for years in her power. During her residence at Vellenaux she had every want supplied, and was safe in her position. With the only evidence of the fraud that had been practiced in her own keeping; she had outwitted him and had in reality obtained the best of the bargain. The knowledge of this cut him to the quick and he detested her in consequence.

Yet his only chance of obtaining that which he so coveted was by an offer of marriage, not that he intended to fulfil any such promise, quite the reverse, it would be a lie, a villainous deception, but had he not willingly defrauded Miss Effingham out of her property? and what was one lie, more or less, it would be but diamond cut diamond, and turning the tables on Mrs. Fraudhurst. All these thoughts flashed through his mind as he sat gazing out upon the sunny landscape below him, if it must be done, as well now as at any other time, perhaps better. He at length arose, and after taking two or three turns up and down the apartment in order to nerve himself for action, stopped beside the chair of the fair widow.

"Eleanor," said he, laying his hand on her arm. She looked up quickly, for he had never before so addressed her. "Eleanor, you are unjust to me and to yourself, ask yourself have I ever deceived or broken faith with you since our compact after Sir Jasper's death, and the answer must be in my favor. You may say that I have acted coldly and kept aloof from you: this I grant is true, but it has been forced upon me; I felt that the eyes of the world were upon us, watching our actions. Your constant residence here has been talked of and cavelled at by some of the neighboring families, who have not recovered from the surprise they felt on hearing that Sir Jasper had died intestate and left his orphan niece unprovided for. It was to prevent exposure that I have thus acted towards you, and I believe that I have effectually succeeded, and now I acknowledge that the charm of your society has become almost indispensable to me, and I will no longer be held back by the world's opinion. Listen to my proposal, accept it or reject it as you will, I make it with all sincerity. Place the will of the late baronet in my hands, and before this day month you shall be my wife and mistress of the the manor."

"And should I survive you," she said, "Vellenaux and its broad lands—"

"Reverts to Miss Effingham on condition that she allows you five thousand per annum and a suite of apartments in the west wing, during the remainder of your life, which you can have fitted up to suit your taste and convenience without delay, in case the contingency you mention should arise sooner than I anticipate."

"And this you swear to fulfil to the letter," she replied, advancing nearer and fixing her eyes upon him as if to read his inmost thoughts.

"On the day after our marriage I will cause a will to be drawn to that effect, this I swear to do by the honor of knighthood."

Her countenance lit up and there was a sparkling brilliancy in her large black eyes as she said, "I believe you—wait a few seconds and I will prove that I do." She then quitted the room, but did not keep him long in suspense; on re-entering she placed the parchment in his hands, saying as she did so, "Remember I now trust you, but beware how you betray that trust."

He opened the document and glanced over it, to satisfy himself of its authenticity; his legal experience enabled him to decide at once that it was genuine. "Eleanor." he then said, taking her hand, "our interests are now identical, we cannot now but act in concert," and raising her hand to his lips, he bowed courteously to her and left the room by one door, while she passed out at another.

"I have carried my point, thought Sir Ralph as he entered his study, and before this day month I shall have sank both name and title, and be an alien from my native land."

"I have carried my point at last," exclaimed Mrs. Fraudhurst, as the door of her dressing room closed behind her; "before this day month I shall be Lady Coleman and mistress of Vellenaux."

It was late that night ere Sir Ralph retired to rest; before he did so he had determined on his future career. For years he had striven to wrest this document from the widow and now with it in his possession, he lost no time in putting into execution the plans he had for so long a time been maturing. This was to proceed without delay to London, raise as large a sum as possible by mortgaging the Vellenaux property to its fullest extent, then retire to the continent and spend the remainder of his days in foreign travel, halting from time to time at the different cities he had visited during the first years of his married life. For in this mode of living he felt he would be more secure than he could ever hope to be in England during the life of Mrs. Fraudhurst. It is true that he could, by fulfiling his promise of marrying the widow, have sheltered himself from the consequences that might arise should his share of the concealment of the will ever appear, but he could escape this alternative by pursuing the course he had marked out for himself. He was aware that a desperate and revengeful woman like Mrs. Fraudhurst would leave no stone unturned to bring about the ruin of the man who had thus deceived and tricked her; but the old lawyer knew that she was almost powerless to act against him with any chance of success, as the only two persons interested in the matter were, to the best of his belief, in India, and likely to remain there for some years at least, and the only real proof that a will had been made by the late Sir Jasper Coleman, was now in his possession, viz: the will itself, and her unsupported testimony would not be taken as evidence in any court of law; besides, in the transaction she was in the eyes of the law the more culpable of the two, being the chief instigator of the plot, therefore it was in a more complacent frame of mind that Sir Ralph, early the following morning, ere the self-satisfied widow had awakened from those slumbers that had been during the night partially and pleasantly disturbed by means of her coming greatness as the wife of a Baronet and the Lady of Vellenaux, had driven over to Switchem and taken his seat in the up train for Southampton, in order to consult with the lawyer who had the management of his estate. After effecting this he started for London.

He was not naturally a bad man at heart, and had he not been legal heir to the baronetcy he would never have entered into the conspiracy to deprive the rightful owner of the property. He had always been of the opinion that the late Baronet would make a will leaving the principal portion of his property to his niece, but fancied that he would come in for a couple of thousand a year, to enable him to support the title; but finding that his name did not appear in the will, he felt both disappointed and annoyed beyond measure, and quite ready to acquiesce in the proposal made him by the intriguing ex-governess.

It was not his wish or intention from the first that the will should be destroyed, and he had certain scruples of conscience which now prevented his so doing. During his journey by train he argued the subject mentally. "They are both young," he thought, his mind reverting to Miss Effingham and Arthur Carlton, "and will, in all probability, survive me many years; let them buffet the waves of fortune in their youth, as I have done, they will then better appreciate their accession to fortune than they probably would have done, had they come into it at an earlier stage of their life; besides, who has a better right, during his lifetime, to enjoy the estate, than the heir to the title. The will must, of necessity, be found among my papers after my decease, so all will come right in the end," and with this consoling plea he settled himself snugly among the cushions of the first-class carriage of the train that was now leaving Southampton far behind, on its upward course to London, and soon fell into a doze.

In another carriage were seated two gentlemen conversing in a very lively and animated strain, and were apparently much interested with scenery, farm houses, and well trimmed hedges, as the train whirled past. They were not foreigners by any means, decidedly English in every look and action; about eight and twenty and thirty, respectively, and very good looking; the tallest was decidedly handsome; he was dressed in grey tweed of fine texture. They had entered the carriage at Southampton. A man of the world would have pat them down, from their general appearance and the well-bronzed hue of their features, as either belonging to, or having served in, the military or naval service of their country; and he would not have been wrong, for they were none other than Captain Carlton and Assistant-Surgeon Draycott, of H.M. Light Dragoons, just arrived from India on furlough.

"We are going along at racing speed," said Draycott to his companion, "but it will hardly keep pace with your impatience to reach London. Gad, I envy you the possession of so fair a bride. I remember the first time I met her at Calcutta. I thought her the most loveable girl I had ever seen; but what chance had a poor devil of an Assistant-Surgeon, only just arrived in the country, surrounded, as she was, by a set of fellows old enough to be her father, it is true, but with rupees enough to freight a Pattima? I suppose that ride through the Goozeratte did the business for you? She is just the girl to admire that sort of thing."

A suitable reply rose to Arthur's lips, but very different words escaped him.

"What the devil is that? A collision, by thunder!" exclaimed he, as he picked himself up from the opposite seat on which he had been thrown by the violence of the shock. The door, fortunately, had been forced open by the concussion. Our two travellers jumped out on to the track. Here a scene of confusion met their view. They had run into a freight train which was coming from an opposite direction. Women and children were shrieking for help, mingled with the cries of those injured, with the loud shouts and vociferations of the employees, and those engaged in clearing the wreck and getting things into trim again; although a number were hurt, some slightly, others more seriously, there were none reported actually killed; and a great number of the passengers were more frightened than hurt.

"This way," said an official to some four or five men, who were carrying a gentleman that appeared to be more seriously injured than any of the rest. "Lay him down softly on that grassy bank;" then raising his voice called out, "Is there any medhal man at hand?"

"Here, Draycott, although on leave you must come to the rescue. Horrid bore to be thus detained, is it not," said Arthur, as they hastened to the spot.

"Fall back there, men, fall back; give the gentleman more air, and let the doctor pass." At the decided and authoritative tone of Carlton's voice the crowd, who by this time had gathered around the sufferer, gave way. The surgeon went to work immediately and examined the unfortunate man thoroughly. "Bad case," he said in a whisper to Carlton. "Broken thigh bone, ribs crushed, and something worse internally, I am afraid." At this moment Carlton got a good look at the features of the injured man. "Can it be possible! Yes, it is Sir Ralph Coleman!" At the mention of his name the Baronet opened his eyes and, for a second or two, looked fully at the speaker, then said with a great effort, for pain had hitherto kept him silent:

"Yes, Arthur Carlton, it is I. How came you here? Do not leave me." And here Sir Ralph fainted from loss of blood.

"Is there a public house or farm near?" enquired Carlton.

"Yes," replied one of the bystanders, "there is farmer Wheatley's just down there in the hollow; they will do what they can for the poor gentleman."

"I will pay the men well that will carry him there," said Carlton, addressing a number of farmers' men, who had by this time come up. The rank of the injured man, and the offer of payment, had a wonderful effect. A dozen volunteered, at once. A gate was taken off its hinges, and some of the cushions of the injured carriage placed upon this litter and, under the direction of Doctor Draycott, Sir Ralph was conveyed to the farm house in the hollow.

"You seemed to be well acquainted with my patient," said Draycott.

"Oh, yes. He is Sir Ralph Coleman, of Vellenaux. He succeeded to the title and estate on the death of Sir Jasper, Miss Effingham's uncle, by which she was left almost penniless. You have heard her history, I suppose, in India. These things always leak out somehow or other in the service."

"In that case, my dear fellow, I must go no further than the door with you. To the best of my belief he will not live more than eight hours, and I must have other opinion and advice in his case. I think it would be as well to have the clergyman and a lawyer without loss of time. He may have something of importance to communicate to you or Miss Effingham ere he dies, for I have some indistinct notion that I have heard something very unfavorable spoken about the said Baronet, now I hear the name again. Let him be got to bed as soon as possible. What is the name of your nearest town, and the distance to it?" enquired Draycott of the farmer.

"Fallowfield is about two miles from here, sir. There is a good road and no one could miss it," was the reply.

"Let me have a horse and I will go myself and get what I require; Captain Carlton will remain until I return," and the young surgeon was soon on his way at a hand gallop. In the meantime the good people of the farm were doing all in their power to render the sufferings of their wounded guest as little painful as possible; and every attention was shown him. He spoke but little; but several times asked for Carlton, and on seeing him only repeated, "Do not leave me yet, Arthur, I may have something to say concerning you and Miss Effingham."

In less time than could have been expected, Draycott returned, accompanied by the best surgeon in Fallowfield, the rector, and a lawyer of good standing in that town. Again the patient was examined, after which a consultation was held in the farmer's parlour, which lasted about a quarter of an hour; the medical men then returned to the bed-chamber.

The Baronet scrutinized their features narrowly as they re-entered the room. "Oh!" said he, breathing with intense difficulty, "I see there is no hope for me; but tell me frankly, how long is it your opinion that I can live?"

"Doctor Draycott and myself," replied the surgeon from Fallowfield—who being much the senior took the lead—"deem it expedient that you should send for your man of business as soon as possible," thus evading the direct question.

Ralph passed his hand across his brow and remained silent a few moments. "You may do so, but it is too late I am afraid. Get the nearest lawyer you can, but be quick for my strength is failing fast, and send Captain Carlton to me at once."

"Arthur," he continued, as the young man advanced, "I have deeply wronged Edith and yourself: in the breast pocket of that coat yonder is a paper packet, bring it to me." Arthur obeyed and placed it on the counterpane. Ralph laid his hand upon it and said, "There is yet time to make restitution. This is the will of the late Sir Jasper Coleman, stolen from his desk on the morning of his death. Has the lawyer sent for yet arrived? If so, I will give my deposition on oath, ere it is too late: I am not a principal, but an accessory. After the fact—" Here Sir Ralph fell back on the pillow, and remained motionless several minutes, during which time the rector and lawyer had been summoned from the parlor below. The rector being a magistrate undertook to put a few questions to the dying man before he gave, his testimony. When sufficiently recovered to speak, the baronet, in a husky voice, related the whole of his interview with Mrs. Fraudhurst, her production of the will and the compact entered into between them. The document was sworn to, signed and duly witnessed by those present.

"Arthur give this will into the hands of Miss Effingham, or her legal adviser, and obtain her forgiveness for me." This the gallant soldier faithfully promised to do. The room was then cleared of all except the rector and the dying baronet. He lingered until sometime after midnight, and ere the light of another day dawned, his spirit had passed away, and the baronetcy became extinct.

During the following day Mr. Russell, the agent, arrived, and Arthur, in the name of Miss Effingham, authorized him to settle all claims, and have the body of the late Sir Ralph conveyed to Vellenaux for interment. Having thus arranged matters, Captain Carlton and his friend Draycott started by the next train for London.

# CHAPTER XV.

It was by no means an uncommon occurrence for Sir Ralph to absent himself from home for a day or two without communicating to any one his intentions or the direction in which he was going, therefore his absence at the dinner table in the evening did not excite any misgivings in the mind of Mrs. Fraudhurst, but his non-appearance at the breakfast table the following morning caused considerable disquietude to that amiable person. Hurried on by her ambition she had aimed at too high a prize, and in so doing had let slip the reins of power. The possession of the will was the only hold she had ever had on the baronet and now when too late she perceived, to her dismay, the awkward position in which she stood. Ever suspicious of the motives of others; she now tormented herself with apprehensions concerning his absence, and the business that could have taken him away at that particular time. From the servants she could gain no information regarding his movements; but it occurred to her that old Bridoon, the gate-keeper, could throw some light on the subject, and therefore determined to lose no time in questioning him as to the direction taken by his master.

The person who had been despatched to Southampton to summon Mr. Russell, the agent, found the gentleman in question had gone to Vellenaux, and thinking from what he had overheard that it was a matter of considerable importance, made no longer delay in that good town than was actually necessary, but took the first train to Switchem, and from thence on foot to the lodge gates, and walked quickly up the avenue; when near the lawn he encountered Mrs. Fraudhurst, who, noticing him to be a stranger and in haste, accosted him and enquired his business.

"I am looking for Mr. Russell, my lady," was his reply.

"He resides in Southampton; but where have you come from, and who is it that wishes to see him?"

"Sir Ralph Coleman, my lady, has met with an accident about two miles from Fallowfield, and is not expected to live long. He has sent for his agent, and I have been to Southampton, but was told that I should find him here."

The widow started and turned deadly pale. "He has the will with him," she thought.

"I beg pardon, my lady, for being so abrupt,—perhaps you are Lady Coleman," for he noticed her start and change color.

"Pray go on, my good fellow, and tell me all about that accident, where the baronet is, and who is with him, and all you know concerning this sad affair."

The man related all he knew, and something that he had heard. "The gentleman that sent me for Mr. Russell they called Captain Carlton." At this name she again started, and, in spite of herself, trembled perceptibly, but the man went on—

"There was something said about a stolen will, which Sir Ralph wanted to enquire about, or something of that sort, and I am in great haste."

"Stay one moment. Did you say Sir Ralph was not expected to live?"

"The doctors said he could not last more than a few hours."

By this time she had recovered her presence of mind. "Mr. Russell," she said, "was here this morning, but has returned to Southampton; you must have passed him on your way here; return my good fellow as quickly as you can, and let him know all that you have told me." She gave him a sovereign and said, "I will be there almost as soon as yourself."

The man took the coin with a bow, and started for the railway station, and Mrs. Fraudhurst returned to the house, where she well knew Mr. Russell then was settling home matters with the steward. She went directly to her own apartment to form plans of immediate action. "Arthur is in England, Sir Ralph dying, the will found in his possession; he has made a confession of the whole, implicating me; he must have done so, or how could that messenger have heard of the stolen will. Idiot that I was, to trust it out of my own keeping. My only safety is in instant flight. I must place the wide waste of waters between me and the consequences that must inevitably await me should I remain here after the disclosure becomes known throughout the country." She then commenced to pack up her wardrobe and valuables. Her plan was soon arranged. She then descended to the drawing room and rang for old Reynolds, who answered the summons. "Has Mr. Russell left the house?" she enquired, and on receiving an answer in the negative, desired that he might be informed that she wished to speak to him, "and return yourself, Reynolds, for I have something of importance to communicate to both of you."

In a few minutes the agent entered, she requested him to be seated. "Reynolds, you too will remain;" then addressing Mr. Russell said, "I have just received the intelligence that Sir Ralph has met with an accident, by rail, resulting, I am told, in a broken limb, which may detain him for some days at the farm house where he now lies; he has requested me to attend him, and bring such things as I may deem necessary, and further directs that you will call over and see him sometime to-morrow." She then gave orders to the butler to pack up several changes of his master's linen, and underclothing in a large trunk and have it sent to her room, as she had bandages, flannel, and other things that it might be necessary to place therein. This was accordingly done, but as soon as alone she emptied the trunk of its contents, and filled it with her own apparel. The carriage was then ordered round, the trunks put in, and Mrs. Fraudhurst, who had found a home there for upwards of twenty years, left Vellenaux never again to return to it.

"She has baggage enough for the Seik men of a whole troop," remarked Bridoon as she passed through the Park gates.

On arriving at the station her first act was to dismiss the carriage, the next to take a ticket for Exeter, and in a snug hostlery in that city made an addition to her toilette, then ordered a cab and proceeded to the principal bank.

"I wish to see the manager," she said, with a condescending smile. The obsequious cashier led the way to the sanctum, and ushered her in, for he knew the visitor well, and also knew that opposite her name in the books of the establishment there was an array of figures, representing a goodly amount of the current coin of the realm.

In about ten minutes the lady, accompanied by the manager, returned, and presented a cheque for the full amount of her deposit, which was paid in gold and notes. This circumstance did not much surprise the banker, for she had done the same on three or four occasions during the last seven years, re-depositing the same amount a few hours after. She was then politely bowed into her cab and was driven off. Having settled her bill at the hotel, she drove down to the railway station and procured a ticket for Queenstown, Ireland, and by the time Mr. Russell arrived at the farm house to attend Sir Ralph, Mrs. Fraudhurst was airing herself at the Cove of Cork. Her object in misleading the man who had been sent to acquaint the agent with what had occurred to Sir Ralph, had thus been effected: that of gaining time to enable her to quit the country before steps could be taken to arrest her.

"There is not a finer craft swims the ocean than the beauty that lays out yonder," said a weather-beaten old seaman to a group of sailors, watermen, and others, who were lounging about the dockhead and commenting on the merits of a first-class, clipper-built, full rigged vessel that was lying in the Cove, her sails loosed and the blue Peter or signal for sailing, flying at the fore.

"You may well say that with your own purty mouth, for it's yourself that knows that same, Cornelius O'Donovan, for wasn't it yourself that made the first trip in her, and isn't Captain Costigan a blood relation of your own, and sure a smarter boy than him that has the handling of her isn't to be found between this and Bantry Bay."

"It is her fourth trip to the Cape of Good Hope," resumed the first speaker, knocking the ashes out of his pipe, and preparing to refill it. Just then a lady, dressed in the height of the prevailing fashion, advanced, and of one of the party enquired the name of the ship, and the port to which she was bound.

"The 'Kaffir Chief,' outward bound for the Cape of Good Hope," was the reply of the waterman who had been addressed. "Shall I put you on board, my lady?"

"Not at this moment,—but when does she sail?"

"She will up anchor and top her boom at sunset," answered another of the bystanders.

"They are lowering a boat," said the old tar, who had first spoken, who was now taking a squint at her through a small pocket telescope; "it is the skipper coming ashore for his papers, mails, and perhaps to jack up some stray passengers."

"You would oblige me by telling the Captain that a lady wishes to speak to him as soon as he lands, and then see if you can manage to drink my health at yonder little public house," and Mrs. Fraudhurst here held out a crown piece to the old seaman, who gladly accepted the offered coin. "What did you say the Captain's name was?" It was immediately given. "Then be good enough to tell Captain Costigan that he will find me waiting for him beneath those trees yonder," she said, as she turned and walked in the direction indicated.

"Pretty spoken woman that; devilish good looting, too; what can she want with old Castigan?" remarked one of the party.

"Missed her passage in the last ship, perhaps, and wants to know if there be any room in the 'Kaffir Chief,'" replied another of the bystanders, "Go over at once to the 'Jolly Sailor'; I will be with you as soon as I deliver the lady's message, and then we will drink her health," said the old salt who had received the lady's bounty.

"Captain Costigan, of the 'Kaffir Chief,' I believe," said Mrs. Fraudhurst as she advanced from under the trees, from whence she had been watching his approach.

"The same at your service madam," was the reply of the polite seaman, as he lifted his glazed hat and bowed to the person who addressed him.

"I have, unfortunately, lost my passage in the 'Eastern Monarch,' which sailed some days since from London, and am anxious to return to the Cape with as little delay as possible. I noticed in the newspaper that your vessel was bound to that port,—am I too late, or have you room for another?" The Captain eyed her for a moment, and apparently satisfied with his scrutiny, replied:

"I have but few passengers, and there is a first-class berth vacant, with excellent accommodation. You will I trust take a sailor's word for that, as the time is short, and I sail at sunset."

"The truth and honesty of our sailors are proverbial," said the lady with one of her blandest smiles. He then accompanied her to the hotel; here matters were quickly arranged, the passage money paid down, and Captain Costigan promised to call for her, and convey her and her effects on board on his return call. This had been so quietly managed—no agent or go between employed—that no person, not even the landlord of the hotel, was aware of her intentions. He was under the impression that the lady, who occupied two of the best rooms in his house, would in all probability remain there for the rest of the summer. This he judged from what she had let fall during a conversation he had had with her an hour after her arrival, and the worthy man was quite taken aback when she paid her bill, and leaning on the arm of Captain Costigan, left his establishment, to take up her quarters on board the good ship, now lying with her anchor apeak in the offing.

From the quarter deck of the "Kaffir Chief," towards the close of that beautiful summer day, could be seen a magnificent panoramic view of one of the finest harbors in Europe, with the purple-tinted hills of Munster in the distance, and the iron-bound coast standing boldly out on either side, and beaten with the surges which impetuously dashed against the rugged steeps. In stormy weather the billows rolled in from the dark ocean in long arching waves, bursting with a deafening noise on the beething cliffs, and scattering the salt spray hundreds of feet in the air. Then again met the eye the fortifications on Spike Island, Convict Depot, Carlisle Fort, Light House, Camden Fort, Black Point, and the handsome City of Cork, with its bustling streets and its quays and docks, crowded with vessels of all nations, presenting a picture well worth travelling miles to behold. But what a bright change has come over the spirit of the age, since the days of Elizabeth and religious persecution, when Cork was made a howling wilderness, because its inhabitants refused to attend the Protestant places of worship as ordered by law. Verily, in every country, and in every age, mad fanaticism has played such pranks before high heaven as to make even the angels weep for poor humanity. But we live in happier times now, and enjoy that great blessing, liberty of conscience, to its fullest extent.

The wind was fair, and, with every sail set, the gallant bark, on the top of the white crested foam of the rippling waves, floated proudly out to sea, and was soon hull down in the distance, her tall tapering spars fading from view, for the bright orb of day had already sank beneath its ocean bed, and the golden tints of the horizon were fast deepening to the purple shades of night. There were but three other passengers, an old Major of Artillery, a merchant of Cape Town, and a juvenile Ensign of Infantry, going out to join his regiment.

There were no other ladies on board; this was a source of infinite satisfaction to the flying widow, who, from prudential motives, had engaged her passage under the name of Mrs. Harcourt Grenville, and fears for her personal safety were completely set at rest on finding that the news of the accident by rail, which had cost Sir Ralph Coleman his life, had not reached the ear of any person on board, and she, herself, was not quite certain but that her accomplice in fraud might yet survive; if so, her condition was still very precarious, but she argued that he would scarcely recover, or he would not have committed himself by making known to the world his share in the transaction concerning the stolen will, and under the assumed name, and in a distant land, she would be secure from detection. She had no intention of remaining at the Cape; her object was to try her fortune in India, and had only come on board the "Kaffir Chief," as it afforded her the earliest opportunity for evading pursuit. She was well aware that she could easily proceed to India from the Cape in one of the Indiamen that so frequently touched at that port, and so, on the whole, she felt tolerably easy in her new position, and set to work, with her usual tact, to make herself agreeable to the Captain and her fellow travellers. Ensign Winterton she took under her especial protection, which very much flattered his boyish pride; made considerable headway with Major Dowlas, who, by the way, was a bachelor; and never failed to accept the proffered arm of the attentive Captain, when on deck; for although married and on the wrong side of fifty, being an Irishman and a Corkonian, he was not insensible to the charms of a handsome woman some years his junior.

Her account of herself was, that she was the wife of a surgeon at Graham's Town, had been some time in England, and had spent the spring and part of the summer in London, and intended to remain at Cape Town until her husband came for her. She had several thousand pounds, the savings of some twenty years, dressed with excellent taste, and had taken such good care of her constitution, that she looked at least ten years younger than she really was, and felt convinced from all she had heard and read, that she would experience but little difficulty in procuring a suitable husband and establishment in one of the Indian Presidencies, she cared not which, and having no acquaintances in the army, was not at all likely to be recognized as the ex-governess of Vellenaux.

# CHAPTER XVI.

There was another change that had taken place in the little village of Vellenaux which has not been brought to the notice of the reader, and may as well be introduced here as elsewhere, since it must be known sooner or later. The venerable rector who had performed the last sad rites over Sir Jasper, did not long survive his old and esteemed friend. He had been ailing for several months prior to his decease, and had been assisted in his clerical duties by a Curate, a gentleman of pre-possessing appearance; about twenty-eight years of age. He appeared to be eminently qualified for the profession he had chosen, and entered with spirit and energy upon the various duties that now devolved upon him; his quiet and unassuming manner gained him the respect of the whole neighborhood. He read with a clear, distinct tone, and his sermons were such as had not been heard in Vellenaux for many years. He was always welcome whenever he visited his parishioners or attended the sick. He took a very great interest in the Sunday school that had been inaugurated by Edith who had, on leaving the Willows, transferred that responsibility to Julia and Emily Barton, and on her sister's marriage Emily presided over the classes. This just suited one of her tastes and habits, who was ever ready to perform some errand of mercy to the poor and the invalid, and was untiring in her efforts to teach the young children. She had often been thanked by the clergyman for her valuable assistance, without which, he was wont to observe, he scarcely knew what he should do.

When the rector was removed from this sublunary sphere, the Rev. Charles Denham, through the interest of Lord Patronage, whose fag he had been while at Eton, obtained the vacant rectorship. This was considered by the good folks of the district to be a fortunate circumstance, and things went smoothly on as in the good old time. But on the death of her parents Emily Barton, as the reader already knows, left Vellenaux to reside in London. The Rev. gentleman did not know which way to turn; he was sorely puzzled; he had depended so much on Emily that he began to think seriously of the possibility of being able to induce Miss Barton to exchange that name for the one of Denham. This matter had been revolving in his mind for some time past, though he had given no utterance to his feelings, and now she was about to leave that part of the country, perhaps for a lengthened period. "If," thought he, "the Sunday school had Emily at its head, it would materially assist me," and he felt convinced that the rectory, without a wife to superintend it, would be, after all, a very lonely place to pass his days in, would she not consent to undertake the double duties. "I have never spoken to her," he said musingly, as he paced up and down his study, "but I shall, when grief for the loss of her parents will allow her to listen to such a proposal."

On parting with him on the morning of her departure, she was somewhat embarassed at his altered manner towards her. She could not but notice his warm pressure of her hand, and his earnestness of manner, when asking permission to visit her in London.

"My aunt and sister will, I am sure, be always happy to receive you when in London," she quietly replied, and after a moment's pause, continued: "I shall likewise still take an interest in the school, and shall be glad to learn how my little scholars are getting on."

The young rector found it necessary to visit London on several occasions during the next twelvemonth.

In one of the broad gravelled avenues of Kensington Gardens, slowly walking beneath the magnificent trees, the soft mossy grass, yellow and white daisy, bending beneath their footsteps, were two figures,—the one a gentleman dressed in black, with a white clerical neck-tie, the other a lady about the medium height, with pretty features, and decidedly elegant figure, which was set off to advantage by the cut and fit of the pale lavender silk dress she wore. They were progressing slowly towards the gate leading into Hyde Park; their conversation was somewhat interrupted by a knot of passing Guardsmen and other fashionable loungers, to be again resumed when they were beyond ear shot. They continued their walk along the bank of the Serpentine, and could the passer by have peered through the lady's veil, he would have found her face suffused with blushes at different turns in the conversation, but they were those of pleasure, for certainly the crimson flush of anger found no place there. They crossed the Park and passed out at Stanhope gate and turned in the direction of Berkly square.

"You have made me so happy, dear Emily, since you grant me permission to speak to your aunt and brother on the subject nearest my heart," and the Rev. Charles Denham pressed the little hand within his own, made his bow, and walked in the direction of Harley Street, while Emily Barton entered the house of her brother Horace.

There is an old saying, familiar to most of us as household words, which tends to show that the course of true love never does run smooth. Now with all due deference to the talented authority who promulgated this startling announcement, we beg to differ with him on the subject. It may be as he says, as a rule, but our belief is that there are exceptions to this rule, as well as to others; for we say without fear of contradiction, that the loves of the pretty Emily Barton and her very devoted lover, the Rev. Charles Denham, glided smoothly and sweetly along its unruffled course, until it eventuated in that fountain of human happiness or misery, marriage. On the lady's side there was no stern, selfish parent who would burden the young shoulders, and drive from her path those inmost pleasures so natural to the young and light-hearted, and cause her to lose her freshness and bloom, by attending solely to his whims and wishes, or crush her young heart with hope deferred. There was no ambitious match making mother, ready to sacrifice the hearts best affections, in order that she might become the unloved wife of some shallow pated young dandy, with more aristocratic blood than brains, and a coronet in perspective.

Nor was the reverend lover subjected to any trials of a similar nature; he was an orphan, with but one near relative, a bachelor Uncle, who was fond of his nephew, and proud of his talent and the position he had attained as Rector of Vellenaux. The old gentleman had intended to leave him his property, amounting to some five thousand pounds, in the five per cents., at his death; but the kind-hearted relative on learning that his brother's son had secured so estimable a lady for his wife; belonging to a family who for so many years had resided in the neighborhood of Vellenaux, the scene of the young Rector's labours; he altered his will, placing half of the original sum to Charles Denham's credit, at Drummond's Bank in London, subject to his cheque or order, so that the rectory could be furnished and fitted up with all the requisites befitting the position of the young couple.

It was a right joyous group that gathered around the wedding breakfast table at 54 Harley Street, on that bright summer morn, that saw Emily Barton made the happy bride of the equally happy Rector of Vellenaux. A friendly Bishop tied the connubial knot in one of the most aristocratic churches in London, and a few hours afterwards Emily and Charles departed, not by rail, to some uncomfortable foreign hotel, but by travelling, carriage and post horses to their home at Vellenaux. For the guests who had assembled to witness the wedding ceremony, there was another treat in store, they were invited to a ball given in honor of the occasion by the brother of the bride, at his mansion in Berkly Square, concerning which more anon.

The term for which the Willows had been rented, now expired, and Horace determined to no longer delay his departure for Devonshire. This had been ever in his mind while serving in India. He loved the old place and there were now fresh inducements for him to give up the house in London, and repair to the Willows. His brother Tom was married and settled at Vellenaux, and Emily had just become the wife of the rector, and lived within a stone's throw of her old home. Thus, with the visits of his aunt and the Ashburnham's, Pauline would not be without society; besides he would take her and Edith, whom he now looked upon as a sister, to London during the height of the gay season, and this he thought would not fail to please all parties.

Mrs. Barton was to give a farewell entertainment prior to her departure, which should exceed anything that she had hitherto attempted, and the evening of the day of Emily's marriage was fixed for the occasion.

It was somewhat late in the afternoon when Captain Carlton and Doctor Draycott reached London, where the two friends and travelling companions parted—Draycott for his father's house in Finsbury Pavement, and Carlton for his hotel in Bond Street. His first idea was to go direct to Berkly Square and inform Edith and the Bartons of the death of Sir Ralph, and the declaration he had made concerning the will of the late Sir Jasper; but while waiting in the coffee room of the hotel, looking over the morning paper, he chanced to hear the following conversation between two gentlemen standing at the bow window that looked out on the street.

"And so the Bartons give their farewell spread this evening? Are you going?"

"Well, I rather think so," was the other's reply. "It is a thousand pities, however, to bury that lovely woman, Miss Effingham, in the country. There is not her equal in town. If she only had a decent allowance of cash or other property, she would have been sought for by a Coronet, you may depend on that."

"But I heard," continued his friend, "that she was engaged to an Indian Officer, who is expected in England shortly," and with these words they passed out into the street.

On hearing this, Arthur determined to defer his visit a few hours longer. There was a great rush of vehicles that night on the South side of Berkly Square. The heavy family carriage, with its sleek horses, driven at a sober pace by old John, the dashing curricle and smart barouche, with the elegant private cab with its busy little Tiger in top boots, whose single arm stops the thorough bred animal when his master drops the reins.

"Is them 'ere hangels," enquired the butcher boy of his crony, Tom Drops, the pot boy at the Crown and Sceptre, just round the corner, as the two young ladies, who had acted in the character of bridesmaids in the morning, stepped from their carriage on to the Indian matting which had been stretched across the pavement to the hall steps, all tarletan and rose buds, and ascended the grand staircase leading to the ball room.

"Well, if they ain't they ought to be," was the response of Tom Drops. At this moment a very stout and elaborately turbaned Dowager passed slowly from her brougham along the matting and entered the hall.

"Is she a hangel too, do you think? Don't look much like one now," enquired the young butcher.

"In course not," said Tom, "they loses all the hangel when they marries, leastways so I have heard. But who it this swell? he is bang up to the mark; he's a horse sojer I knows, and a ossifer," as the embroidered sabretache of

Captain Carlton met his view while ascending the hall steps. "Well, I am off," said one to the other and the two lads went their way.

"Show me into the library, and hand this card to Miss Effingham," said Arthur to a servant at the foot of the staircase. The footman first looked at him, then at the name on the card, then said, with a low bow, "Certainly, sir, certainly," and ushered the Captain to rather a snug little apartment which was used as a library. Edith was dancing when the footman entered. On the conclusion of the waltz he approached and quietly handed her the card. A flush of pleasure lit up her beautiful features, and joy sparkled in her brilliant eyes, as she read the name, and without a word to any one, followed the servant and passed straight to the room where her lover waited for her. We will pass over the transports of their first meeting,—it can be easily imagined, as the reader, is already aware of their engagement, and that he had returned to England for the sole purpose of their union. After the emotion of the first few moments had subsided Arthur related to her the accident by which Sir Ralph had been killed, and of the existence of her uncle's will, and the way it had been stolen by Mrs. Fraudhurst, and Sir Ralph's complicity in the plot.

A feeling of regret at the untimely end of the unhappy man, as he had been hurried into eternity without preparation, came over her for a few moments, this was chased away by indignation at the fraudulent and base part that had been played by her late governess and companion. "What has become of her?" she inquired.

"Decamped, and no doubt fled the country ere this; all that is known of her is that she left Vellenaux on the plea of rendering all the assistance in her power to Sir Ralph, but she did not make her appearance in that neighbourhood," was Arthur's answer. The reader knows more of her movements than any of her acquaintances at Vellenaux or London.

"And we shall have dear old Vellenaux to live in. Oh! Arthur dear, I am so happy, with all the friends I hold most dear on earth residing around us. You will of course leave the service now? How kind of my poor, dear uncle to think of us both in his will. But Mrs. Barton may notice my absence, and become uneasy, so let us return;" and in another moment or two, leaning on the arm of her handsome affianced husband, Edith re-entered the ball room, much to the relief and surprise of Pauline Barton. Arthur Carlton took an opportunity during the evening of relating to Mr. Barton the change that had taken place in Edith's circumstances by the death of, and disclosures made by, the late Baronet.

"Meet me at breakfast in the morning, and we will consult as to what immediate steps should be taken on this extraordinary occasion; but of course you will sleep here," said Horace. Arthur assented, and was soon again at Edith's side, who had told confidentially to Mrs. Barton all that he had told her: and that little lady could not restrain her delight, and before eleven o'clock that evening, every one in the room became aware that the beautiful Miss Effingham was worth twenty thousand pounds a year as heiress of Vellenaux.

Mr. and Mrs. Denham, previous to the ball, took their departure for Devonshire, and were comfortably settled in the Rectory before Horace returned to the Willows. He had postponed their journey in order that Arthur and Edith might have the benefit of his advice and assistance in such matters as might arise during the establishment of their claims, set forth in the will of the late Sir Jasper, now produced.

Mr. Septimus Jones was a lawyer of good repute, carrying on his practice now, and had been doing so for upwards of fifteen years in the main street of Hammersmith leading to the Suspension Bridge.

"Nicholas," said that gentleman one morning, as he laid on his desk a copy of the *Times* newspaper, which he had been carefully perusing for upwards of an hour, "Nicholas, do you remember a youth named Edward Crowquill, that I had in my office some ten years since?"

The old and confidential clerk ceased writing, and thrusting his pen behind his ear, rubbed his hands softly together, and said, "Most certainly I do. He was not fit for the business, and gave it up through ill health; studied medicine for a time, and is now a chemist and druggist, residing some hundred yards down the street."

"Exactly so," replied his employer, "you will be good enough to put on your hat and go and request him to do me the favor to step up here for a few moments." Nicholas did his master's bidding, and returned shortly, accompanied by Mr. Crowquill. Mr. Jones, after requesting him to be seated, and directing his clerk to pay attention, took up the newspaper, and read, in a clear voice the following advertisement: "To Lawyers and otters.—If the party who drew the will of the late Sir Jasper Coleman of Vellenaux, Devonshire, and those who witnessed the same document some ten years ago, will call at the office of Messrs. Deeds, Chancery, and Deeds, Solicitors, Gray's Inn Lane, they will be handsomely rewarded for their trouble." "Now, gentlemen," continued he, "I drew this will, and you both witnessed it. Do you both remember the circumstance." After a little reflection they both recollected the circumstance.

"Oh! since you have not forgotten the occurrence, I will show you a rough draft of the will which I made at the time, and by reading this it will refresh your memories, and you will be better able to swear to the real will if it should be produced."

"When do you purpose calling upon the Solicitors?" enquired Crowquill.

"To-morrow morning we will call for you on our road to town," replied Mr. Jones, politely bowing his visitor out of the office.

# CHAPTER XVII.

Of the early history of Sir Lexicon Chutny very little was known. He was of Dutch extraction that was obvious, had served for a time in the Madras Civil Service, but on acquiring a large property by the death of a distant relative, he retired from that service and settled on one of his plantations in Pallamcotta. How he obtained his title no one knew or enquired, his relative, now deceased, was so called, and in his will he directed that his heir should assume his name and rank. He was thoroughly Indian in his tastes and habits, sensual and self indulgent; saw very little European society, and report said that he had several native mistresses, and was reputed very wealthy. He had never married, for European ladies at that period were rarely to be met with in Pallamcotta. It must have been business of no ordinary importance to induce him to leave the land wherein he had been born, to visit Hamburg, where he made his stay as short as possible. He was not favorably impressed with the Frauleins and fair-haired daughters of Holland, and was now returning home in the "Great Mogul," a Dutch Indiaman bound to Madras.

"Wreck on the lee bow!" shouted a look out from the mast-head. This excited quite a commotion on deck, from whence the object was soon discernable through the telescope, and soon after by the naked eye. The ship's course was altered and she bore down upon the unfortunate craft to render such assistance as might be necessary. She proved to be the ship "Kaffir Chief," from Cork, bound to the Cape; she had been dismasted in one of those terrific storms which so frequently occur in these latitudes, and was now lying completely water-logged on the bosom of the treacherous ocean. The day previous to the wreck had been remarkably fine, but as night closed in the wind rose and continued to increase until it blew a perfect hurricane. In spite of the utmost exertions of the crew the sails were blown clear of the bolt ropes, yards and spars were carried away, when the foremast went by the board and the main topmast fell with a crash into the sea, seventeen of the crew were hurled into the wild waste of waters. A little before daylight a tremendous sea struck her stern, unshipping the rudder, carrying away the wheel, round-house and lockers, rendering her unmanageable, and she was tossed helplessly like a log upon the mighty billows. As the day broke the storm somewhat subsided, a scene of wild desolation was realized by those on board the unfortunate vessel, as the flashes of broad sheet lightning, with which the heavy clouds were surcharged, occasionally shot forth. The scene was startling and terrific, the wild waves were breaking over her and three more of the crew were swept overboard. As the light increased the sea began gradually to go down, and spars and pieces of wreck were seen floating all around, lifted upon the surging waves, to which some of the unfortunate seamen had clung with the grasp of despair, only to be again thrown into the dark trough of the sea to rise no more.

Although the hurricane had subsided, so much water had been shipped that the pumps had to be kept continually going to prevent the hull from going down: to this laborious task all had to exert themselves to the utmost, and only by this means could the ship be kept afloat. The self-styled Mrs. Grenville rendered good service in this hour of peril, she voluntarily took the place of the steward, now called to the pumps, and served out rations of biscuits and spirits to all hands, nor did she forget herself on the occasion. The danger of her position appeared in no way to appal her, and having to undergo no bodily fatigue beyond her strength, she was very little affected by the disasters and hardships of the past few days. Such of the officers and crew as had not been swallowed up by the boiling surf were in a very weak and exhausted condition, owing to their great labor at the pumps, when rescued from their perilous position by the boats of the "Great Mogul." These particulars were gathered from time to time from some of the crew, but from Mrs. Grenville a more detailed account of the wreck was obtained. That lady thought it necessary to keep to her cabin for the first week, during which time she had to sketch out a fresh plan of action for the future.

This she soon effected, having received all the required information from the little fat Dutch stewardess concerning the ship, its destination, and the names and positions of the passengers.

"My dear madam," said the polite Captain, addressing Mrs. Grenville, "you really must allow me to recommend you to try an airing on the quarter deck this beautiful morning; after the long seclusion of your cabin you will, I am sure, find it both agreeable and refreshing." In a graceful manner, and with a pleasing smile, she replied,

"I shall be happy to adopt your suggestion Captain Hanstein, and if it is not interfering with your professional duties, may I request the favour of your arm for a promenade, as I feel scarcely equal to the effort unattended."

The Captain bowed and assisted the lady to the quarterdeck.

The Indigo planter, who had sat opposite Mrs. Grenville at breakfast, felt somewhat annoyed that he had not solicited the pleasure of accompanying the lady in her walk on deck; he had been struck with her appearance at first sight, for the widow knowing the effect of first impressions, had been exceedingly careful with her toilette that morning, and certainly did look her best.

Sir Lexicon had never yet seen any one who came up to his idea of a handsome woman, until he encountered Mrs. Grenville that morning; her curling dark hair, superb neck and shoulders, stately figure and sparkling black eyes, and well modulated voice fascinated him, as no woman as yet ever had done. She was not young, it is true; but this he regarded as fortunate. She was still some years younger than Sir Lexicon; but as to who or what she was he was a stranger; but this he was determined to ascertain if possible, and betook himself on deck for the purpose. As the professional duties of the Captain called him for a time away, he took his place beside the lady and endeavoured to interest her in his conversation. He found her charmingly condescending, and apparently frank and friendly in her remarks, and after about an hour's chit chat allowed him to conduct her to her state room.

Poor Captain Costigan had been killed by a falling spar and knocked overboard. The remainder of the crew and passengers that had been rescued from their precarious situation on the wreck had been on board the "Great Mogul" about a couple of weeks, when she let go her anchor in Table Bay. These, with the exception of Mrs. Grenville, went on shore in the first boat that came off to the ship. She, that morning, had an interview with Captain Hanstein, and some hours after the others had left, the obliging Captain took her ashore in his own boat, in which also sat Sir Lexicon Chutny. He put up at the same hotel as Mrs. Grenville, and was seen escorting her about Cape Town.

The "Mogul" remained only two days at the Cape, then resumed her voyage, and Mrs. Grenville, the Captain, and Sir Lexicon Chutny, could be seen pacing her quarterdeck as she sailed out of the bay, unquestionably enjoying, with much pleasure, the clear, balmy, and exhilarating breeze of the early day, which, with the assistance of the sun's rays, was lifting from the table land on the summit of the great mountain, called occasionally Table Rock. A large, heavy, white cloud that frequently spread itself over the whole surface, resembling very much in appearance an enormous table cloth, hence the origin of the name. This remarkable mountain is steep, rugged and precipitous, and towers up hundreds of feet towards the clear, blue vault of heaven. Very little brushwood or vegetation is to be found thereon. At its base, snugly ensconced under its protecting shade, is situated Cape Town, looking quite pretty and picturesque as the day dawns and the rising sun appears. There are two other smaller elevations in close proximity to the Table Rock, not without interest, and called respectively the Lion's Head and Lion's Rump, possibly because they are connected together by a ridge of rock, which, to the imaginative mind, gives it the appearance of an enormous lion, sleeping. The other objects of interest and the shipping in the harbor were soon left far astern.

As they were sweeping out to sea, the Captain could, by the aid of his glass, clearly distinguish the signal that was flying from the flagstaff, situated on the lofty eminence mentioned before, as the Lion's Rump signalling station, announcing the approach of an English vessel from London. On hearing this the lady's face changed to an ashen hue, and she trembled slightly. It was for an instant only; her strong will conquered the emotion, and with her feelings now under perfect control, she was again conversing and smiling in the most charming manner until luncheon was announced, to which she was conducted by Sir Lexicon, and while thus engaged she felt that she had good cause to rejoice that a fine swelling breeze was carrying her rapidly away from the Cape of Good Hope; for, doubtless, the newspapers brought out by the new arrival, contained a full account of Sir Ralph's death, and her own flight from the country, and it was quite possible that some suspicion might have fallen upon her, had she remained a day longer at Cape Town.

The wealthy planter of Pallamcotta was not the only person on board who had become infatuated with the lively widow; for in fact Captain Hanstein, the honest-hearted seaman had been caught in her toils. He had believed every word that had been confidentially told him by Mrs. Grenville, her position in life, and her reason for visiting the Cape and Madras. Of course there was scarcely a grain of truth in the whole statement. She was not long in discovering the Captain's weak point, and rather encouraged him than otherwise, but had no notion of engaging herself to the fat honest Dutch skipper. Far from it, but she thought it necessary to her project to mislead him on that point. This unscrupulous and ambitious woman cared not how she wounded the feelings of others, if she thought by so doing it would further her own interest. She was determined to secure Sir Lexicon as a husband, and thus become Lady Chutny; and so skillfully did she angle, and played her cards with such great tact, that there was very little doubt of her succeeding.

The Dutch are naturally slow of action, and the planter's wooing was of a rather passive character, and his attention to the lady did not excite the suspicion of her other admirer, who did not think it would be necessary to pop the momentous question until she was about to leave the ship on reaching Madras. That Sir Lexicon was somewhat piqued at the marked attention paid to her by that good-natured sailor was quite evident, and was exactly what the widow had anticipated and desired. She played both lovers off, one against the other, and the result proved that her theory and practice were correct; for Sir Lexicon took advantage of an opportunity that was afforded him one afternoon while playing chess with Mrs. Grenville in the after cabin. They were quite alone, and during a pause in the game, he formally made her an offer of marriage, which, after a little skillful beating about the bush, she accepted, but on the condition that nothing should be said about the subject to any one on board. This was agreed to, and the game continued. There were other passengers on board, but, as they are in no way connected with our story, it would be needless to particularize them.

On the vessel reaching her destination, the gallant Captain mastered up courage, and boldly and in a straightforward manner, asked Mrs. Grenville to become his wife. The lady listened to him with polite attention, and said in reply:

"Captain Hanstein, I should be very sorry if any act of mine has led you to believe that I looked upon you in any other light than that of a friend, from whom I have received many acts of kindness. I regret to pain you by a refusal, but it must be so, for I now tell you in strict confidence that I am engaged to Sir Lexicon Chutny." Then with a smile and a graceful bend of the head, she left the bewildered Captain to his own reflections; and shortly after, attended by Sir Lexicon, quitted the ship.

After a sufficient time for procuring all the necessary paraphernalia considered indispensable on such occasions had elapsed, the marriage was celebrated in the Cathedral at Madras, and the ambitious views of the mercenary woman were at length realized. "She could" she thought "play the great lady in Pallamcotta, and somewhat astonish the good folks at the Capital by the brilliancy of her entertainments periodically, for Sir Lexicon, although self-indulgent, was by no means of a miserly turn, and would, for a time at least, feel a certain pleasure at the admiration that would be excited by the splendour of her ladyship's assemblies."

Their stay at the Capital, on this occasion, was but of short duration, as Sir Lexicon was anxious to return to Pallamcotta to finally arrange the business that had taken him to Hamburg. To this arrangement her ladyship made no objection, it suited her views exactly; her idea was, that her advent in India should become known to the gay and fashionable butterflies of the Presidency as quietly and gradually as might be. It was necessary that they should be aware there was such a person as Lady Chutny in existence; but for the present she would be heard of only and not seen, so that when she appeared among them and threw open her splendid rooms for balls and other entertainments it would be considered a matter of course, a thing to be expected from the wife of so wealthy a man as Sir Lexicon was reputed to be. Her ladyship's theory was the correct one, for by acting in this manner she would be relieved from the hubbub and cry of "Who is she?" and "Where does she come from?" that would consequently follow, should she at once rush into the vortex of fashionable life. She had no intention of burying herself at Pallamcotta, now that she had attained the position for which she had risked so much. She had played her cards boldly and unscrupulously, and, during the shuffle had twice nearly come to ruin; but she had now, she believed, won the odd trick that would secure her the game, and she resolutely determined to hold on to the stakes thus acquired. From the retrospect of her past life she turned herself steadfastly away, and looked only into the brilliant future, which she fancied was opening before her. What was there to fear? There was no one in India who could recognize her, or knew anything of her antecedents. Edith and Arthur had returned to England; restitution had been made and justice done them by the unlooked for death of Sir Ralph Coleman. He was the chief culprit; she merely an accessory, acting under his direction and guidance; and, now that she had placed oceans between her and the scene of their crime, nothing, she argued, could transpire to mar her triumph, and, laying this flattering unction to her soul, her ladyship prepared for her journey with a buoyancy of spirit that astonished even herself.

Lady Chutny found the establishment at Pallamcotta very different from what she had anticipated. So unlike the Bungalows of rich civilians at the Capital, where all was order and quiet, and the gardens well kept. Here everything was slovenly and in confusion, only a small quantity of the furniture that had lately arrived from Madras had been unpacked, and this was strewn about the drawing-room and sleeping apartments without the least attempt at arrangement. The Bungalow had been originally a very handsome one, but from indolence and carelessness had been allowed to fall into a partially dilapidated state. The only covering to the floors of the large, handsome apartments was the common matting of the country. The same was the case in the broad and spacious verandahs, up to which the rank vegetation of the compound—for garden there was none—spread their creeping fibres in wild luxuriance. But her ladyship offered no ungracious remark on the state of things, but simply requested her husband to summon the whole of the servants and, in her presence, inform them that she was their mistress, and to be obeyed in everything, without remark or hesitation. This was done, and in forty-eight hours she had completely revolutionized the whole establishment.

Fifty of the plantation hands were employed in clearing up the compound, forming a garden and a lawn, while the edges of the verandah were lined with pots of the most magnificent plants and fragrant flowers that could be obtained, and before she had been in her new home one week, everything was in complete order.

She had heard it reported previous to her leaving the capital that Sir Lexicon had several native mistresses at his different plantations, and by her ayah or lady's maid, a Madrasse who could speak English, these stories were confirmed, and she determined to govern herself accordingly, fully believing that her husband would have the good sense to remove any such persons as might be at the Bungalow in Pallamcotta before her arrival. Caring nothing personally for Sir Lexicon, it gave her little or no concern whether he chose to keep native ladies at the other plantations or not, but she certainly did not intend that any of them should reside under the same roof with herself, therefore she was much annoyed and disgusted to find that her husband had not thought it necessary to give any orders concerning their removal, and she had only been a few days at Pallamcotta, when she learned that there were three Circassian beauties sumptuously cared for and absolutely residing in apartments fitted up for them; though not actually in the Bungalow, they communicated with it by means of a short covered way leading from the back drawing-room.

Taking advantage of Sir Lexicon's absence shortly after, she sent for the head servant, who dared not disobey her orders, and desired him to have the ladies turned out of their quarters and expelled from the premises, and their rooms put to another use.

This was accordingly done and they were afforded shelter and protection at the house of the overseer of the plantation, but at some distance from the Bungalow.

The history of these Circassian girls was anything but an uncommon one in many parts of the country thirty or forty years ago.

Their father, a horse-dealer, had been lured by the glowing accounts of the fortunes that were to be made at the different Presidencies of India, by a traffic in horses, and he determined to test the truth of the reports, and, if possible, to enrich himself by means of his beautiful steeds, of which he had several; but this proved a ruinous speculation, for ere he reached Bombay he lost two of the most valuable, and being totally unacquainted with the tricks and chicanaries so frequently resorted to by Europeans and others in the racing stables and on the turf, he fell an easy prey to some of the sharpers that usually infest the race course, so that by the end of the season he had not only lost every horse that he brought with him, but likewise every rupee he possessed. There were few of his countrymen on the Island, and they either could not or would not assist him to return to Circassia. He had brought with him, to see the wonders of the chief cities of the three Presidencies, his wife and three daughters, the eldest only seventeen, the youngest about fourteen. In his extremity he turned to the old Eastern custom, still prevalent, that of selling his children; he had applied to several European and native gentlemen, with whom he had become acquainted on the turf, but without success. At length he fell in with Sir Lexicon Chutny, to whom he had lost large sums of money during that gentleman's visit to the Island. Here he found no difficulty, Sir Lexicon having seen the beauty of the girls, and being assured by them that, under the circumstances, they did not object to the transaction. He used this precaution, well knowing, although they did not, that he could not hold them to their bargain one moment after the purchase money was paid, should they claim the protection of the police authorities; besides, the poor girls had heard of similar cases to their own, in their far distant home, and thought it must be so elsewhere. So the arrangement was quickly completed, the horse dealer and his wife having accepted the twenty-four hundred rupees, the price agreed upon for their children, departed homeward. Nor did Sir Lexicon delay an hour longer than was actually necessary in the Presidency of Bombay, but hastened with all speed towards his estate at Pallamcotta, in Madras, taking his fair bargains with him.

Here they dwelt in perfect harmony, their lives embittered by no petty jealousies, and wonderfully attentive to their lord and master, over whom they possessed considerable influence when they chose to exert it. There was not a servant on the plantation but would have been discharged had they dared to disobey any orders given by either, whether their master was at home or abroad. For nearly four years this state of things had existed, when lady Chutny's arrival totally altered the aspect of everything, and created quite a hurricane of passion in the hitherto quiet household, by driving the favorites forth with flashing eyes, hatred in their hearts, and thirsting for vengeance on their hated rival.

Lady Chutny had resided at Pallamcotta some six or seven weeks, and began to think that the term of her probation had lasted quite long enough for the purpose for which she had immured herself in the country, and at length determined to visit the Capital. Her husband had successfully, though unwittingly, paved the way for her reception among the *cream de la cream* of society; being a man of wealth, and likewise a sporting character, he had the privilege of the entree to many of the best houses in the city, and was always hand and glove with most of the staff and other officers, both military and naval, who were glad to welcome him at their mess-room or club-houses. Like a child with a new doll, he was proud of his handsome wife, and could not refrain from dropping a word here and there concerning her. The old Bungalow had, under her direction, been restored to its ancient splendour. It was her ladyship's intention to come up to town shortly, and give a series of balls and receptions, when she would be much pleased to receive his friends; and by this means Lady Chutny's advent among the big bugs at Madras, was quietly heralded without the slightest effort or ostentation on her part.

# CHAPTER XVIII.

The firm of Deeds, Chancery and Deeds, of Gray's Inn Lane, the Solicitors employed by Horace Barton, on behalf of Miss Effingham, and who had caused to be inserted in the *Times* newspaper the advertisement alluded to in a previous chapter, had not long to wait for the information sought after. For on the following morning Mr. Septimus Jones, Mr. Crowquill and the firm clerk, presented themselves at the office in Gray's Inn Lane. The rough draft was produced, and the will of the late Sir Jasper Coleman, brought to London by Arthur Carlton, and now in the hands of the Gray's Inn lawyers, compared with it, and after careful scrutiny it was declared to be the identical will drawn by the Hammersmith lawyer, and witnessed by his two clerks several years ago; this was duly sworn to, and certain other documentary evidence taken down, and the three gentlemen returned to their homes in Hammersmith, each twenty guineas richer than when he had left it in the morning.

Now, although there was no one to contest the will, yet there were certain legal technicalities and forms to be gone through before Edith could take formal possession of Vellenaux, besides these same lawyers had been empowered to draw up the marriage contract, settlements, etc., between her and Arthur, the doing of which would take a considerable time, much longer perhaps than the ardent lover might think necessary. Edith would not hear of her dear Arthur remaining in the service after their marriage; so arrangements were made for the selling of his commission; this sum, together with the amount bequeathed to him by the late Sir Jasper, would put him in possession of seven thousand pounds.

It was planned that the wedding should take place at the old fashioned church at Vellenaux. There was to be no wedding tour, but the bridal party and a large number of friends were to proceed to Castle Audly, the seat of Lord De Belton, who had served in Arthur's regiment, and had been intimately acquainted with him for a few years in India. Castle Audly was a very ancient and romantic pile, and quite the show place of the country, here there was to be a magnificent *Fete Champetre, Dejeuner a la fourchette*, with archery and other amusements provided by the noble owner; the whole party were to return and dine at Vellenaux, and wind up the entertainment by a grand ball at night.

"Of course, my dear Carlton," said Horace Barton to that young gentleman one afternoon while lounging in the drawing room in Berkly Square waiting to attend the fair Edith in a canter through Hyde Park, "of course you will stand for the county at the next general election? Sir Sampson French, who is too old to again take office, will, I am certain, retire in your favour, if you will only come forward as a candidate; you have plenty of friends and admirers in and around Vellenaux to ensure your return if properly canvassed. A man of your ability and standing in society cannot afford to remain idle at such a time, though he may have a rich wife to back him."

"I should like to get into Parliament above all things, and certainly shall endeavour so to do, providing Edith gives her consent, and the good folks of the county will give me their support," was Arthur's reply as the lady of his love made her appearance equipped for the ride.

It had been the intention of the Bartons, to return to Devonshire immediately after, the ball in Berkly Square, but the sudden appearance of Captain Carlton with the startling announcement of the accidental death of Sir Ralph Coleman and the disclosures made by the unhappy man ere he breathed his last, caused them to put off their intended departure for some weeks, until matters were *en train* for establishing the validity of Edith's claim to the estate of her late uncle.

Aunt Cotterell and her good humored husband had, without the knowledge of any of their friends, built a handsome house on the bank of the brook which ran between Tom Bartons and the rectory; besides this, Mrs. Ashburnham had confidently whispered to Cousin Kate that her dear William was about to give up his practice which, for the last fifteen years, he had labored at so assiduously and successfully, and that he was now actually arranging for the purchase of that very pretty villa and grounds just beyond the Willows, as its owner, Sir Edmund Wildacres had, by racing and other gambling proclivities, managed to run through and overdraw his cash account at his bankers, so that his landed property had to come to the hammer, and, the young spendthrift was about to retire to some cheap Continental watering place until some of his antiquated relatives should be condescending enough to shuffle off this mortal coil and resign their purses and property to his careful control. And with Edith and Arthur settled at Vellenaux, there would be formed at once a happy circle, bound together by ties of family affection and disinterested friendship, and with such supporters as these to canvass his cause, Arthur's return, as County member, might be looked upon as amounting almost to a certainty.

The lovers did not fail to take advantage of the extension of time to be spent in the great metropolis, and balls parties, operas, and galleries of the arts and sciences, exhibitions of pictures and such other amusements as best suited the tastes and inclinations of these two, for the time being, devoted votaries of pleasures, were visited. There was another most important matter that had to be attended to, and this was one that entailed numberless visits to and from Madam Carsand's in Bond street, Store & Martimer's, Waterloo Place, and other fashionable emporiums, where the numerous articles, indispensable to the trousseau and toilette of a young and beautiful heiress.

It will be remembered that in the search for the Begum of Runjetpoora, Carlton had brought away with him in his sabretache a small steel casket as a trophy; after his return from the fort, and while dressing for mess, he remembered this circumstance, and was about to open and examine the casket and had already taken it in his hand for that purpose, when footsteps were heard approaching the tent, and not wishing others, to see his little prize he carelessly tossed it into an open trunk, among his wearing apparel, where it remained undisturbed until after his arrival in England, when, in looking over his wardrobe he came across the identical casket which had lain there so long and by him quite forgotten. Unable without the key to open it himself, he sent for a locksmith, who, in a very short time caused the lid to spring open, when, to Arthur's surprise and delight it was found to contain a number of precious stones of great value, in fact it was the Begum's jewel case, containing diamonds of the first water, rubies of unusual size, and pearls of great price, which, on being taken to a jeweler, proved to be worth, somewhere about ten thousand pounds. Arthur, although by no means a man of business habits, knew enough to convince him that this sum, together with the five thousand pounds left him by Sir Jasper Coleman, with what might be realized by the sale of his commission, if properly invested, would secure to him an income of not less than twelve hundred a year, a very pretty sum for a man to have of his own for pocket money, although his wife should happen to possess twenty thousand a year. He determined to carry out this arrangement as soon as any suitable opportunity for so doing came to his knowledge, but with the exception of Draycott he told no one of the Begum's jewels, or his intentions concerning their disposal.

# CHAPTER XIX.

The happy, light Dragoon, in order to be near the lady of his love, had taken up his quarters at Harold's Hotel, in Albermarle Street, a very quiet, but aristocratic place, leading into Picadilly. Beyond the Bartons and their family circle, he had few intimate friends, in fact, except Draycott, the surgeon of his regiment, with whom he had been on the most intimate terms for years in India, and to whom he revealed all his joys and sorrows, there was not one male friend he cared a jot for in London; of course the men of his club, and those he had met abroad, who, like himself, were now home on leave, dropped in upon him occasionally at his rooms; but his constant visitor and companion in his peregrinations through the labyrinths of the great Babylon during the height of a London season, was Draycott: he was young, clever, high principled, thoroughly good natured, and of an old county family. He had but once only paid a flying visit to the metropolis previous to joining his regiment in India, and now having a few pounds to spare, was determined to enjoy himself in the gay Capital to his heart's content, and whenever practicable, induced Arthur to give him his society.

They had been breakfasting together, one morning in the latter's apartment, and were discussing numerous scenes and things at home and abroad in which they had both participated; nor was Arthur's approaching marriage with Edith Effingham, and his idea of leaving the service, left uncommented upon by his old friend.

"Well," remarked Draycott, with a gay, good natured laugh, "after your adventures and hair-breadth escapes, together with your great good luck in winning the beautiful heiress, it would not surprise me in the least if some old fairy godmother dropped from the clouds and transformed you into a gallant young Prince of some beautiful isle of the sea, yielding untold wealth, like the isle of the famous Count de Monte Cristo." Here the conversation was interrupted by the entrance of the waiter, who handed Arthur a card, which announced that a Mr. A.G. Capias, of the firm of Docket & Capias, Solicitors, Bedford Row, desired to speak with him on business of a private character.

"More parchment and red tape work cut out for you to-day," remarked the surgeon, "so I am off, but will drop in later in the day."

"Now, my good fellow, oblige me by remaining where you are until this matter—be it what it may—is disposed of, and I will then stroll out with you," said Carlton. Then, turning to the waiter, said, "Show the gentleman up at once." The obsequious attendant bowed and withdrew.

In a few moments the door was thrown open, and a spruce, dapper looking gentleman, clothed in sombre colored garments, irreproachable linen, and carrying a small merino bag in his hand, was ushered in.

"I believe I have the pleasure of speaking to Captain Arthur Carlton of H.M. Light Dragoons," said that individual, as he advanced towards the table, at which the two friends were seated.

"Late of the Light Dragoons," replied Carlton, "for I have sold out—or, what amounts to the same thing, I have directed the Army Agent to do so"—pointing as he spoke to a vacant chair.

The man of law availing himself of this piece of politeness took the chair, placing his bag on the carpet at his feet.

"And what may be your pleasure or business with me? You may speak out," said Carlton, noticing the glance that his visitor threw at the surgeon, "that gentleman is my most intimate friend and brother officer."

"I have a few questions to ask concerning your father and grandfather, the answering of which may lead to something, I have no doubt, will, at no distant date, prove of much importance to you and yours," was the reply.

"Proceed then," said Arthur, "with your interrogations, and I will reply to the best of my ability, though I must candidly confess that I know very little of the early history of my father, and still less of my grandfather, for they both spent so many years abroad, in India and on the European Continent."

Mr. Capias hereupon drew from his bag a small bundle of letters and papers and arranged them on the table in front of him, then commenced his enquiries as follows:

"Will you be so good as to state the name and position of your father, his place of birth, the school or college where he was educated, and the place of residence at his decease."

"Arthur Howard Carlton, Colonel of Cavalry in the service of Her Majesty, born at Montazuena, in Mexico, educated at Rugby, and died at Exeter, Devonshire, England, in the fifty-sixth year of his age, leaving but one son, your obedient servant," here Arthur bowed in a somewhat stately manner to his, interrogater.

"Exactly so," said the lawyer, glancing at a paper he held in his hand, which he then placed on the table, and taking up another, said:

"Will you now tell me all that you know concerning, your grandfather?"

"He was called Eustace Vere Carleton, I believe, from the fact of his signing himself so in his letters to my father, wherein he desired that he should enter the British service, and said that he should provide his commission and make him a small yearly allowance as long as he remained in the service,—these two letters are now in my possession and at your service, should you require them," so saying, Carlton took from his desk the papers in question, which he handed to the Lawyer. "But, pray, sir, in what way and to what extent am I to be benefitted by the early proceedings of my paternal relatives?" enquired the Dragoon, darting at the same time a knowing wink at the surgeon, who at that moment happened to look up, for until then he had appeared to be deeply absorbed with a late number of *Punch*, though in truth he was very much interested in, and had not lost a word of the conversation that had been going on between the lawyer and his friend Carlton, but he only shook his head in acknowledgment of the friendly wink, and continued to turn over the pages of that comical but highly interesting periodical which he had taken up at the commencement of the interview.

"Every lost link in the chain of evidence is, I believe, now complete," replied Mr. Capias, "and I am at liberty to communicate to you the following circumstance which, doubtless, up to the present time you have been a stranger to." He hereupon cleared his throat, and in a well modulated voice said:

"Maud Chumly, your great grandmother, the daughter of a Church of England Clergyman, at the age of eighteen married Arthur Eustace Carlton, ninth Earl of Castlemere. The result of their union was a son, a wild, harum scarum sort of a youth who, at the age of nineteen, was provided with an appointment and sent out to the British Embassy at the Court of Spain. While here he managed to get entangled and elope with the wife of a Castillian Hidalgo; they were pursued and overtaken by the enraged Grandee and his followers; the lady was recovered, but the husband lost his life in a duel with the gay Lothario who, subsequently, to avoid the vengeance of the family and the strong arm of the law, fled to Mexico, where, a few years after, he married the daughter of a French officer of high rank, by whom he also had an only son, but never returned to England, nor did he, on the death of his father, assume the title or take possession of the estate, but resided continually on the Continent; nor did he by word or deed reveal to his beautiful wife or child his real position in the Peerage of Great Britain. His son at an early age was sent to England, and was educated principally at Rugby, but he also graduated at Cambridge; he afterwards entered the English army, and during his stay in India married the daughter of a Judge of one of the native courts, and like his father and grandfather before him, had but one son, his wife having died during her passage to England. The bereaved officer served, subsequently, with great distinction, through the Peninsular Campaign, became Colonel of his regiment, and at the close of the war was placed on half pay, and at the age of fifty-six, died at Exeter, in Devonshire; this only son, Arthur Carlton, likewise entered the army and became a Captain of Light Dragoons, and is now beyond the possibility of a doubt, the rightful and lawful heir to the late Earl of Castlemere." Here Mr. Capias bowed most deferentially, gathered his papers together, said that he trusted in a few days to have the honour of another interview with his lordship, and then vanished from the room.

"The fairy Godmother, in the garb of a limb of the law, by all that's wonderful," burst forth Draycott, who was the first to speak after the visitor had departed.

"The next lady presented to her Majesty, by her Grace the Duchess of Opals, was the lovely and accomplished Edith, Countess of Castlemere, on her marriage with the noble Earl of that name." "By jove! it sounds well," exclaimed Arthur, starting out of a reverie into which he had fallen, and springing to his feet. "Draycott" continued he, "am I awake? Can it be all true what the little man in black has been telling us?" and Carlton paced excitedly up and down the apartment.

"Not a doubt of it, my lord," resumed Draycott "these musty old lawyers never commit themselves by letting out so much as this one has done, unless they are quite sure that everything is all safe, cut and dried and ready for use, as the saying is, and I think your lordship cannot refuse to join me in drinking the health of the future Countess of Castlemere;" and, suiting the action to the word, filled out two bumpers of sherry, which he and Carlton, nothing loath, quaffed off.

"And now for the stroll. I must call at the Bartons and mention this piece of news to Edith; but, my dear fellow, not a word of it at the clubs. Of course, they will hear of it from the newspapers before the world is many hours older."

Arthur was right, for the *Pall Mall Gazette*, of the following day, announced the retirement from the service of Captain Carlton, Light Dragoons, by the sale of his commission, and the *Court Circular* of the same date created quite an excitement in fashionable circles by the following: "*On dit.*—Captain A. Carlton, late of the Light Dragoons, has just succeeded to the title and estates of his great grandfather, the late Earl of Castlemere, which title had lain dormant for several years, in consequence of the only son of the late nobleman never having assumed the title, and died in obscurity abroad, and we, learn that the new Earl is about to lead to the hymenial altar the beautiful Miss Effingham, heiress of the splendid estate of Vellenaux in Devonshire."

The news of the alteration in Carlton's social position was received with the utmost satisfaction in Berkly Square. Edith was too firmly convinced of the unalterable attachment of her lover to fear that a change of fortune would, in any way, alienate or weaken the love he bore her, believing, as she did, that

Arthur loved her with all the devotion of a long tried affection. Certain alterations in the programme had to be made, consequent on the elevation to the Peerage of the Bridegroom elect. The wedding, which, was to have taken place in Devonshire, was now to be celebrated in London; this entailed a delay of some few weeks in order that the family mansion of the Castlemeres, in Saint James' Square, might be re-decorated and furnished in a style befitting the occasion.

As the rent role of the Carlton Abbey property produced an income equal to a clear ten thousand a year, Arthur now considered himself in a position to carry out the great desire of his heart, that of presenting to his beloved Edith the costly gems he had brought with him from India. He therefore took them to one of the leading jewelers in London for arrangement and re-setting, and among the beautiful and costly wedding presents from the aristocratic connections of the Earl, from the Bartons and others who had known Edith from her infancy, there were none that could compare in any way with the magnificent diamond tiara ear rings and bracelets, the cross rings and brooches of rubies, pearls and diamonds, from the jewel case of that mutinous Indian Princess, the Begum of Runjetpoora.

With such zeal and good will did the lawyers on both sides work, that in less than three months from the death of Sir Ralph Coleman, Edith was in possession of Vellenaux, and Arthur had been recognized and installed as Earl of Castlemere, and master of Carlton Abbey, that being the name of the estate in Nottinghamshire, where the old Earl died.

Having thus succeeded to the title and estates of his forefathers, Arthur quitted his rooms in Albermarle Street, and located himself at his mansion in St. James' Square, which, although undergoing extensive alterations and decorations, had still a sufficient number of apartments in thorough repair and handsomely enough furnished, to satisfy the taste of a more fastidious person than our ex-Light Dragoon. It was really astonishing the number of visitors he had to receive, and cards and notes of invitation were showered upon him from people whose very existence he had previously never heard of, connections by marriage of the past generation crowded upon him, mothers with marriageable daughters invited him to their assemblies, young men of his own order sought to engage him in the various pursuits considered indispensable among those by whom he now found himself surrounded. When it became generally known that the new Earl was, beyond the possibility of a doubt, engaged to be married, the connections just mentioned thought it right and proper to recognize in Edith Effingham the future Countess of Castlemere; and, on learning that she was the niece of a baronet, and heiress, in her own right, to twenty thousand a year, she was sought after and made much of by the aristocratic relatives of her affianced husband, for the privilege of entering, as honoured guests, such places as

Vellenaux and Carlton Abbey was not to be lost for the want of a little tact and polite attention to the bride elect, and so Edith's circle of female friends enlarged rapidly, and it was from among these that she selected the eight young beauties who were to act as bridesmaids on her marriage day, now fast approaching.

The Bishop of Exeter, who had been well acquainted with Arthur's father, offered his services on the interesting occasion, which were gladly accepted. Exactly at 11 a.m., the family carriage of the Bartons, containing Edith, Pauline Barton, and three of the bridesmaids, left Berkly Square. In a second were seated the other five ladies acting in that capacity. Then came the large, roomy vehicle of the good natured stock broker, occupied by Mr. and Mrs. Cotterell, Horace Barton and Mr. and Mrs. Denham, who had come up from Devonshire expressly to be present at the ceremony. Tom Barton and Cousin Kate accepted seats in the handsome barouche of the Ashburnhams.

The cavalcade reached Westminister Abbey just as the Bishop of Exeter, attended by two other clergymen, drove up. Quite a number of aristocratic equipages, with their occupants, had already arrived, and just as the bride was descending from her carriage, a handsome cabriolete, driven by the Earl of Castlemere; attended by his groomsman, Draycott, dashed up at full speed. Quite a large assemblage had gathered about the cloisters and aisles of the venerable structure, where it had pleased Miss Effingham to have the marriage solemnized, all anxious to get a glimpse of the wedding party, as they moved up to the chancel and took the positions assigned them in front and to the right and left of the altar, and a fairer scene than the one now presented to their view, had, by many been rarely, if ever, witnessed. The warm, ruddy light of a summer's sun, subdued by the gorgeously colored panes of the magnificent oriel windows above the altar, fell softly, yet brightly, on the richly dressed groups that composed the bridal party.

Attended by a bevy of young maidens, Edith, in the pride of her womanly beauty, now fully matured and developed, advanced with a firm step and knelt before the altar, her symmetrical and perfectly faultless figure appearing to advantage in a rich white corded silk, with its superb train of the same material, the whole trimmed with fine old point lace of the most costly description; nor did the exquisitely worked veil she wore conceal the tresses of golden brown hair that fell in luxuriant ringlets on her alabaster shoulders. The magnificent diamonds of the Begum encircled her fail brow, neck and arms, while pendants of the same precious stones hung from her small, shell-like ears, their brilliant prismatic hues shooting forth and glittering with lustrous and dazzling brilliancy at each movement of the wearer; but far brighter than all was the glorious rays of the light of love and joy that danced and scintilated in the deep blue eyes of the bride as she stood forth and plighted her troth to him she so fondly and devotedly loved, and the face of the handsome Earl beamed with unclouded happiness as he placed the small golden circle on the finger of his future Countess.

The ceremony was not a long, but an impressive one. The bridal anthem was beautifully rendered by the choristers, accompanied by the clear, full, deep tones of the grand old organ. As the clock in the square tower was striking twelve the whole party left the Abbey, and were driven to the Earl's mansion in Saint James' Square, where a luxurious repast was prepared for them, to which ample justice was done. At two, the Earl and Countess stepped into their traveling carriage and were whirled off to Brighton, from which point they were to start on their bridal tour through Continental Europe.

The Bartons and Cotterells left town a few days later for their homes in Devonshire, where they hoped to be comfortably settled ere the honeymoon of the happy couple should have terminated, as it was the desire of all concerned to give them an enthusiastic welcome on their return, and arrangements and preparations were at once entered upon to make the occasion one of general rejoicing and festivity, and a general holiday to all in and around Vellenaux.

# CHAPTER XX.

The city of Madras, the seat of Government and Capital of the Presidency of that name, although not possessing all the facilities for an agreeable sojourn to the lover of pleasure and amusement that may be found at the capitals of the sister Presidencies—Bengal and Bombay—it having neither the healthy climate of the one, or the wealth of the other. Yet there are times and seasons when Madras is very enjoyable: just after the south-west monsoons, when all nature is clothed in verdant beauty, and a delightful coolness pervades the air, the Neilgerie Hills cannot be surpassed by those of Mahableshwa or any other sanitary station in India, even the Capital itself, whose shores are washed by the boiling surf from over the triple reefs of rocks during the rainy season; but that time being past, a more tranquil state of things pervades the ocean, and cool sea breezes waft over the city. At the time of which I am writing, Madras was more than usually gay, several vessels of war were in port and a number of crack corps had arrived from Europe and elsewhere, officered by a set of men whose fathers and great-grandfathers before them had served their country either in the army or navy; they served not for pay but for honor, and to uphold the high and honourable name bequeathed them by their ancestors. Many of these came into the regiment not to save but to spend money, and it was surprising to the calculating natives the enormous sums they managed to get through during their short stay at any of the large towns or stations where Europeans do most congregate.

The stream of fashionable life was now at its height, now in full force when Lady Chutny's magnificent bungalow was thrown open for receptions; and it was not long before the fame of her ladyship's fetes and assemblies spread far and wide. Sir Lexicon was known to be exceedingly wealthy, and it will be remembered that Mrs. Fraudhurst, on quitting England, had drawn out of the bank her capital of ten thousand rounds. This sum, together with a large amount given her by the planter for the express purpose of giving entertainments in town, had been paid into the bank of Madras, in Lady Chutny's name. The sum was actually only one lae and a half of rupees, but dame rumour, with her hundred tongues, had quadrupled it.

The season was now at its height, and her ladyship had issued cards for an entertainment that was to exceed anything before attempted in Madras The spacious verandahs to the right, left and rear of the bungalow were converted into lounging halls, half drawing-room, half conservatory, while the compound and gardens were brilliantly illuminated with countless colored lamps and lanterns. Hundreds presented themselves for admission to the fairy-like scene, and it was allowed by all to be a perfect success, a gem of the first water of entertainments, and such, as many of the guests had seldom witnessed. Her ladyship, elegantly attired, and flushed with pride and pleasure at the triumph she was achieving moved gracefully about from one room to another attending to the comfort and convenience of her visitors. In passing along one of the improvised conservatories, the figure of a cavalry officer attracted her attention. His features were screened from her view by the leaves of a magnificent orange tree, but there was something in his general outline, as he stood leaning indolently against the trellis work chatting with a drawl, real or affected, to a little lady seated, or rather reclining on a low ottoman close by, something that caused her to start as if the gallant officer was not altogether unknown to her, but her memory would not at the moment serve her, yet a feeling of mistrust, a sort of almost indescribable sensation of disquietude came over her as she listened to the polite nothings that issued from his lips; but fearing to attract observation she quietly withdrew, and entering the upper end of the ball room summoned her chobdah and pointing out the figures said, "When that gentleman leaves his present position, tell him that Lady Chutny desires to speak with him." The native made his sallam and withdrew. In a few moments the object of her enquiry advanced towards her, and without preface or introduction, commenced, "I am informed that your ladyship has done me the honor to request my presence, and, like an obedient slave, I am at your ladyship's command," and he bowed with the most deferential politeness as he delivered himself of this harangue; then recollecting for the first time that he had no card of invitation from, or introduction to, her ladyship, began to stammer forth his excuses, that he had dropped in on the strength of having met Sir Lexicon for a few minutes at the mess of the Fusiliers, and had accepted his general invitation as a *carte blanche*. He was quickly relieved from his embarassment by his handsome hostess declaring herself fortunate in numbering among her friends so gallant a chevalier. "I was not aware that your regiment was in town, nor do I believe that I have ever met your distinguished corps, and it was to explain away the seeming slight in neglecting to forward cards that I have requested a few minutes' conversation with you."

"Your ladyship is kindness itself, and our fellows will duly appreciate your affability on reaching Madras; for, unfortunately for them, we are still quartered at Secunderabad. I alone am here on court martial duty and have, I fear, intruded upon your hospitality. But I believe I have had the pleasure of meeting your ladyship before, though I must confess that when and where has escaped my memory; unpardonable in me, certainly, to forget the occasion that introduced me to so charming a lady." They were standing opposite one of the large mirrors, and by a skillful manipulation of her fan, the hostess contrived to obtain a perfect view of the features of the gentleman who was now addressing her, at the same time revealing but little of her own. For a few moments she too was mystified as to who he was, or under what circumstances they had met, or whether it was a case of simple mistaken identity; but another searching glance at the mirror, and the truth flashed upon her in an instant. Her thoughts travelled back to Vellenaux. Yes, it was he, the same Snaffle of the Lancers, who had figured as young Lochinvar at the fancy dress ball, and had subsequently lunched there on one or two occasions during the shooting season, prior to Arthur's joining his regiment. She felt certain that he had not as yet recognized her, but that he must do so at length she felt convinced. To be recognized by him after so many years was an event which she had not calculated on. It was one to be dreaded, for, doubtless, the disclosures that he could make, would bring her to disgrace and ultimate ruin; but she was equal to the trying ordeal.

"If we have met, my dear sir," she said, in a low, soft voice, "it must have been at the Cape, or in London. Although I do not think that your regiment was in either of those places during my residence there, but that circumstance need not prevent us from becoming better acquainted." He bowed and retired, and the smiling hostess moved among her guests as though nothing had occurred to disturb her. On the following morning the card of Captain Snaffle was handed to her, but she excused herself from appearing on the plea of indisposition. The sight of the Lancer's card both startled and alarmed her. He had discovered her identity with the ex-governess of Vellenaux, or he would never have presented himself at so early an hour after the bail. What was to be done? She must return at once to Pallamcotta, and an hour after the gallant Captain had left, she quitted her bungalow. She need not have been so much alarmed, for, although Snaffle, who, during the evening, had obtained a good look at her unobserved, it was not until late in the morning that he remembered her as the companion of Edith at Vellenaux. Nor had he heard anything of Sir Ralph's death, or the crime which had caused her to fly from England, but this she did not know, and as "conscience makes cowards of us all," she sought the refuge of her bungalow at Pallamcotta.

With agitated feelings, and distracted with doubts and fears, it was in no enviable state of mind that Lady Chutny re-entered her home on the plantation. Judge then of her indignation to find that during her absence the favourite mistresses had been re-established in their old comfortable quarters, for, while she had been amusing herself at the Capital with balls and parties, they had regained their ascendency over Sir Lexicon, who, not expecting her ladyship's return for several weeks, had consented to their returning to the bungalow until suitable arrangements could be made for them. He ladyship's sudden and unexpected return, together with her order for their immediate expulsion, aroused their passions—which during her absence had remained dormant—to intense hatred, and they were determined to sacrifice her at the altar of jealousy and revenge, and resolved to execute their wicked project without further delay. Sir lexicon's absence, they well knew, would afford them an excellent opportunity for carrying out their design. The servants, they were sure, would act in concert with them, by affording them the facilities they required.

"Gopall," said one of the three, "bring the Madam Sahib's food into my room before you place it on the table this evening." "And," responded another, "I wish to act as her ayah, and carry the sherbet to her chamber tonight. You understand, eh? You shall have a gold mohur from us." The butler grinned with intense satisfaction, for he had no doubt of their intentions, and his little black eyes twinkled with delight at the idea of receiving the gold coin promised; and at once gave the assurance that they might count upon his assistance, and likewise the co-operation of the other servants.

During dinner Lady Chutny enquired whether her orders regarding the three women had been attended to, and if they had left the house. The crafty butler pretended not to understand the meaning of her words. She could not speak the language, and her ayah, who had always acted as interpreter, whenever she wished to issue her commands personally, had been, owing to her hasty retreat, left behind at the Capital. Boiling with rage at being, as it were, set at defiance in her own house and by her own domestics, fatigued with her journey, and alarmed at the prospect of being in the power of Captain Snaffle, also dreading the disclosures he might make, it was no wonder that she sought the quiet of her own chamber much earlier than was her usual custom. For several hours she turned uneasily on her couch, her mind disturbed by conflicting doubts and fears, when a strange attendant entered, bearing a large goblet of sherbet, which had been rendered deliciously cool by being placed for several hours in a mixture of saltpetre and glauber salts. This was her favourite evening beverage, which, in her now heated and excited state was very acceptable. Motioning the woman to place it on the teapoy, near her pillow, she was about to give her further instructions, when she noticed that she was a stranger, not from her features, for they were concealed beneath the folds of her sarree, which had been thrown completely over her head, revealing only a small portion of the lower part of her face, but from her general appearance. Finding that she was not understood, she stretched forth her hand for the goblet and took a long draught, unconscious of the piercing dark eyes that gleamed down upon her with jealous hatred and fiendish pleasure from behind the silken sarree of her new attendant, as she took from her hand the half-emptied goblet, which, after placing on the teapoy, she quickly left the room. There was something suspicious about the action of the woman, but Lady Chutny was too much occupied with her own thoughts to notice it at the time, and soon after sank into a doze from which she started in affright, as if from some dreadful dream, only to fall into another. This occurred several times. At length, after finishing the remainder of the sherbet, she dropped into a deep sleep.

The sun was high in the heavens when she again awoke. A burning fever consumed her, and delirium had fastened on her with fearful spasmodic and excruciating pains internally. She endeavored to rise, but fainted in so doing. She shrieked wildly for assistance, but none heeded her cries. For hours she was thus, left alone, the pains increasing, and her brain in a constant whirl. Again she slept, how long she knew not. When, on awaking, she found the same attendant who had waited on her the previous evening, standing at her bedside. She had brought food, of which her ladyship partook slightly but eagerly, and called for tea, which was handed her.

"Has Sir Lexicon returned," she enquired. The attendant shook her head. "Send for him immediately, and likewise a doctor. I am in great agony." The woman muttered something, and left her. Through the long, lonely hours of that dark night, the wretched woman, wracked by intense pain, with insanity steadily gaining the ascendency, tossed to and fro on her weary bed, and when overtaxed nature did succumb to slumber, wild dreams, and wilder fancies haunted her between sleeping and waking. She fancied she saw at her bedside the forms of Edith, Arthur, and Ralph Coleman. The latter she denounced as a coward and traitor, from Carlton she hid her face, but to Edith she stretched forth her hand and implored her to save her from the torments she was now enduring, but only meeting with a scornful laugh, fell back upon her pillow exhausted.

This had not been quite all fancy, for the three mistresses of the planter had stolen into her chamber to feast their cruel eyes upon the dying agonies of their helpless victim. Towards the middle of the fourth day, reason had somewhat resumed its sway, and the violence of the pains she had experienced were subdued, the ayah had arrived from the Capital and now resumed her attendance upon her mistress. She had sought out the native doctor who attended the sick of the plantation. He, although in the pay of the three women, thought it best to visit Lady Chutny when summoned.

"Is there no European doctor?" enquired the patient, as the native practitioner felt her pulse and otherwise examined her.

"No, madam, but I will ride to the next station and endeavour to procure one," replied the crafty little man. Then turning to the ayah, said, "I should have been called in sooner. The Sahib must be sent for without delay," and after leaving a few instructions, left the room. He knew that death must soon ensue, and was determined to be absent on Sir Lexicon's arrival under the pretence of doing all in his power to procure European medical assistance. As he passed through the women's apartment he said to them, "I am going for a European doctor. Of course, I shall not find one. You understand? You have done your work completely. She will die at sunset. You had better send for a missionary or priest, and have her buried as soon as possible. Let the grave be dug under the palm trees, on the south side of the plantation, and have all done decently and in order, and the master will attach no blame to any one or have any suspicion that foul play has been used, then you can easily persuade him to allow the body to remain there."

The native doctor was right. The unhappy woman never saw the rising of another sun, and in the white sands, beneath the waving palms, where the hyena prowled and the wild jackall barked hoarsely through the night, lies the mortal remains of this ambitious woman, who thus fell a victim to the jealous and revengeful passions of those by whom she had been surrounded by her unscrupulous husband.

The third day after the ball, Captain Snaffle again presented himself at Lady Chutny's bungalow, and was informed that her ladyship had left town, and would, in all probability be absent some weeks. The fashionable world was in a great commotion at this unexpected event. They could not understand it. To leave town at the height of the season, and just as she had achieved so great a triumph as her last ball was allowed to be, it was quite inexplicable. It was talked of, canvassed over, and commented upon, at the band stand, race course, conversaziones, and mess room, for several days, and, in fact, until the mystery was cleared up by a startling *denouement*.

"I say, Snaffle, old fellow, who the deuce is she? You know, or I am much mistaken. I saw you making great play, and coming it rather heavy with her on the night of the ball. I watched you both for some time. You two have met before under different circumstances. I wager my chestnut mare against your bay colt that I am right. Will you say done?" and Harry Racer, of the Fusiliers, here produced his book in hopes of entering a bet.

"Not quite so fast Racer, my boy. There is no mystery in the matter, no subject for a wager. We have met before, I knew it while talking to her, but could not remember where. I recollect all now. Whether she recognized me or not, I cannot tell. She is a very clever woman. If you will say nothing about it, I will tell you all I know."

"Not I! not I," replied Racer, half despondingly at the prospect of being able to enter a wager in his betting book disappearing.

"Well then," continued Snaffle, "she was a Mrs. Fraudhurst, a widow governess and companion to a rich heiress, niece of Sir Jasper Coleman of Vellenaux in Devonshire. How she got out here, and in what way she managed to hook Sir Lexicon, I cannot imagine, but I will find it all out at our next interview, depend upon it."

"Stop! By Jupiter! Did you say governess, Baronet, name Coleman, place, Vellenaux, Devonshire? Here's a go! Not a word. Here, Ramsammy, bring the fyle of English newspapers from the library, quick." The papers were handed to him, and, selecting *Bell's Life*, Harry Racer commenced reading the following paragraph:—

"Frightful railway accident. Death of Sir Ralph Coleman of Vellenaux, Devonshire. Startling disclosures. Stolen Will. Heiress defrauded. Flight from the country of accomplice, the family governess. Full particulars in our next issue."

"That's her, the planter's lady. Large as life and twice as natural. The thing is as clear as mud in a wine glass. All plain and smooth as a three mile course. The mystery is solved. She recognized you at the ball, saw that you were mystified, but would, doubtless, remember her if you met again. You call the next morning. She refuses to see you on the plea of indisposition. Takes the alarm, bolts off the course, and makes for the open country, where she, doubtless, intends to remain until she hears that you are safe on your road to Secunderabad; and now, old fellow, what are you going to do? There is money to be made out of this matter if you are not too squeamish," and here Racer tipped a knowing wink to his friend of the Lancers.

But Captain Snaffle was a gentleman, and had no idea of trading upon the necessities of others, be they who they might. He merely replied by saying:

"Racer, you will not mention a word of this to any one at present. I will go down to Pallamcotta and find out to what extent Lady Chutny has compromised herself. After that we can decide what is to be done about letting fashionable world into the secret." The two friends left the Fusiliers' mess room, Harry Racer trotting off to inspect some new horses that he had got scent of, and Snaffle to his own quarters.

The following morning saw him on his way to Sir Lexicon's plantation. On the road he overtook the baronet, and they rode the remainder of the distance together. Imagine their consternation on finding that lady Chutny was both dead and buried.

The planter, with his usual indolence and procrastination, was for allowing things to remain as they were. "There is no use," he said, "now, that the matter is all over, of disturbing the body. I will have a handsome monument erected over her remains, and the place shall be nicely laid out with shrubs and flowers, and kept in good order while I live;" But Captain Snaffle thought otherwise. He felt certain that the woman had not been accessory to her own death, but that foul play had been used by some one and he was determined to ferret it out. Immediately on his return to Madras he communicated his suspicions to the police authorities, and enquiries were instituted, a reward offered, and the whole affair came to light.

But it was not until several months after this event transpired that our friends at Vellenaux became aware of the ultimate fate of the ex-governess. Captain

Snaffle, in a letter to Arthur, gave an account of the whole transaction, from which it transpired, that, on enquiries being set on foot respecting Lady Chutny's sudden death, Gopall, the butler, turned Queen's evidence, and confessed the whole of the diabolical plot. Datura, a powerful narcotic poison, had been mixed with the sherbet, this produced delirium, and a quantity of pulverized glass had been introduced into the food given to the unsuspecting victim, which produced inflammation of the bowels, and the combined effects of these caused death. However, the perpetrators of the foul deed unfortunately managed to escape, by what means the writer did not state.

# CHAPTER THE LAST.

Carlton Abbey, the estate of the Earls of Castlemere for centuries back, was situated near Ollarten, on the borders of Sherwood Forest, in Nottinghamshire. It was formerly a religious house of the highest order, largely and richly endowed, whose broad acres ran some distance into "Merrie Sherwood" itself. It is reported that the renowned Robin Hood, with a score of his followers, once sought and obtained shelter and protection there, when pursued by the Sheriff of Nottinghamshire for slaying the king's deer and other misdemeanors within the limits of the forest; and later here also took place the celebrated meeting between Cardinal Woolsey and the Duke of Buckingham, previous to that haughty prelate's dismissal from royal favor and ultimate disgrace, and on the death of the Marchioness of Cosingby who, for forty years reigned as the Lady Abbess, the sisters of this order moved elsewhere, as the property fell into the hands of Eustace, first Earl of Castlemere, heir-at-law, by whom and his successors, alterations and additions were made becoming the home of an English noble; but although the last Earl lived a retired and secluded life, Carlton Abbey was not allowed to fall into decay, and the manor, preserves, and grounds generally were kept in excellent order, and so the Earl of Castlemere, as we must now designate our hero, found it; for on being assured that he was, beyond the possibility of a doubt, heir to the estate, had paid a flying visit to Nottinghamshire, and while there had given orders to the housekeeper and steward to have a handsome suit of apartments prepared for the reception of the Countess and himself; he likewise gave directions to his agent to raise a troop of volunteer cavalry, the cost of which was to be defrayed out of the revenues of the estate, the men to be selected from among the tenantry and well-to-do farmers residing on the Abbey lands.

On their return from the continent, the Earl and his bride took formal possession of Carlton Abbey, received the visits of the neighboring families, inspected the newly improvised cavalry, mustered and feasted the tenantry, and made known to all concerned that they intended to reside, for at least four months in each year, at the Abbey, then took their departure, leaving a very favorable impression behind them.

On the return to London of Edith and Arthur from their wedding tour, they were presented at Court. The Queen seemed to take considerable interest in the handsome Earl and his beautiful Countess, for His Excellency the Commander-in-chief had mentioned to Her Majesty some of Arthur's gallant exploits while in India, and the romantic train of events that had happened to both Earl and Countess prior to their marriage. As a mark of royal favor they were invited to Windsor Castle. This, in itself, was sufficient to give them *eclat* in the highest circles. They gave a series of brilliant entertainments in

Saint James' Square, which hundreds of the highest in the land made a point of attending. Fortunately the London season was at its close; this allowed Edith to carry out her long-cherished wish to return to Vellenaux as its honoured mistress. There were associations connected with it that could not be effaced by all the gaieties of the most magnificent courts of Europe. Arthur too was somewhat tired of the exciting life they had led for some months past, and was anxious to re-visit the quiet spot where the happiest years of his early life had been spent; accordingly they left London for their old home among the beech woods of Devon.

The day of high jubilee, the day of feasting and merriment, such as had never been witnessed in Vellenaux by its oldest inhabitant, at length arrived. High and low, rich and poor of the village and for miles around, turned out in holiday costume to witness the return of Edith and Arthur to their childhood's happy home. Triumphal arches of eve greens and flags had been erected at different places between Switchem station and the Park gates. The two troops of volunteer cavalry that had been raised from among the tenantry of Carlton Abbey and Vellenaux, armed and equipped at the expense of the Earl and Countess, already licked into something like order and discipline by the non-commissioned officers of the regular service, procured through Arthur's interest at the Horse Guards, lined both sides of the road between the arches. Several bands of music, sent down from London, were stationed in different parts of the grounds, and enlivened the scene by playing many of the most popular airs of the day. A deputation of about one hundred gentlemen and well-to-do farmers, all mounted, and headed by the Lord Lieutenant of the County, met the happy couple as they stepped from the platform into their open barouche, with its four prancing and gaily decorated horses, which was in waiting at the Switchem station. After several addresses had been read and replied to, the cortege passed slowly on towards Vellenaux, the cavalry filing in rear and the gay holiday seekers following as best they could. On arriving at the principal entrance the party alighted, the host and hostess, and their invited guests proceeded to the grand hall, where a magnificent collation awaited them. The remainder spread themselves over the grounds and Park, where, beneath the outspreading branches of the fine old trees, were placed benches, beside tables groaning under the weight of enormous sirloins, rounds of beef, and pies of mighty dimensions, with sweet home-made broad, and other edibles of various descriptions. Tents were pitched here and there, where also could be obtained, all free, gratis and for nothing, fine old October ale, rich sparkling cider, clotted cream, curds and whey, tea and coffee, and confectionery in great abundance. Feasting and merriment being the order of the day.

Games of various kinds were entered into with such alacrity and good will, proving how thoroughly they were enjoyed by both participants and lookers on. Cricket, pitching the quoit, and foot ball was going on in one part of the grounds, single stick; and quarter staff playing, and wrestling matches between the men of "Merrie Sherwood," Nottingham, and the yeomen of Devon in another.

There were also foot races and a variety of other amusements taking place in the home park, while the votaries of Terpsichore tripped it gaily on the green, velvety award beneath the grand old oaks; and not a few of the lads and lasses betook themselves down the green, shady alleys to the woods in search of blackberries, or to gather bunches of clustering hazel-nuts. The intimate friends of the lady of Vellenaux amused themselves with archery and croquet on the lawn, and strolled about the grounds watching the tenantry and others in their pursuit of pleasure. All the servants and retainers, for none had been discharged, hailed with delight the return of their young mistress and her handsome husband, for both were alike looked up to and respected for their many amiable qualities, by those among whom they had been brought up since childhood. The two old veterans, Bridoon and Tom the game keeper, had, in honor of the occasion, donned their uniforms and were the big guns of the evening, presiding, as they did, at the upper ends of the tables where the volunteer cavalry were regaling themselves to their heart's content on the good things provided for them.

The day's festivities were closed with a grand display of fire works, and bonfires were lit in many places, which crackled and sent upwards millions of bright sparks, to the intense delight of the juvenile portion of the community. The long rooms in the two public houses, in the village, were thrown open for dancing. The servants' hall, and the two great barns at Vellenaux were also decorated and arranged for the same purpose, and a right joyous time was there kept up, almost until the dawn of day.

Within the time-honoured walls, in one of the superb and luxuriously furnished apartments of Vellenaux, did Edith and Arthur, on this, the first night of their return, entertain the Bartons, Cotterells, Ashburnhams, Denhams, and a large circle of acquaintances. It was not a ball, not exactly a conversazione, but a sort of happy re-union, an assemblage of old friends and familiar faces, many of whom, had, to a certain extent, participated in the joys and sorrows that had attended their host and hostess from their youth upwards, and, as this pleasing picture fades from view, let us take a perspective glance through a pleasant vista of progressive years, at another equally interesting tableaux, whose back ground and surroundings are the same as the previous one. Vellenaux, that magnificent pile of buildings, with its beautiful and varied styles of architecture, embosomed, as it were, in the rare old woods of Devon, its parks and wondrous parterres, its fountains, marble terraces and statuary, all brought out in bold relief by the glorious golden light of a summer's setting sun.

On a spacious terrace of the western wing, whose broad steps of fine Italian marble led down to the clear, open, finely gravelled walk that surrounded a beautiful and well kept lawn, were grouped, in various positions, a number of ladies, gentlemen, and children, with all of whom, the juveniles excepted, the reader is already acquainted.

The Earl of Castlemere, with his beautiful Countess leaning lovingly on his arm, are pacing leisurely up and down among the assembled guests, exchanging here and there words of courteous pleasantry. Lounging over the back of a handsome fautiel, Colonel Snaffle, of the Lancers, is conversing with Pauline Barton, in his usual gay and lively manner, relating to some reminiscence which occurred to them while dwelling on the sunny plains of Hindostan. Horace Barton, Aunt Cotterell and the Rev. Charles Denham were discussing some knotty point concerning high and low church, etc., while some political question was evidently exciting the minds of the worthy old Stockbroker, Dr. Ashburnham, and Tom Barton. The good natured Draycott was exhausting his powers of pleasing by relating to Mrs. Ashburnham, her sister Emily and pretty Cousin Kate, the last *on dit* going the rounds of the fashionable circles at the metropolis.

Light-hearted, happy children gamboled on the broad marble steps, or seated on soft cushions at their parents' feet, listened to the sparkling wit, repartee and agreeable rattle that broke forth among the gay loungers on the terrace. Occasionally the eyes of the whole party would rest with admiration and pride on the scene enacting before them, and well they might, for on the smooth, soft, velvet-like sward of the croquet lawn, eight youthful figures, the eldest scarcely sixteen, were engaged in that most exhilarating, delightful and exciting of all out door amusements, the game of croquet.

The Lady Eglentine Carlton, eldest daughter of the Countess of Castlemere, a tall, graceful girl, inheriting all her mother's soft beauty of form and features, stood with her small, exquisitely shaped foot resting on a bright, blue ball, evidently listening to some suggestion of her partner, Clarence Ashburnham, preparatory to giving the final stroke that would croquet her adversary's ball to a considerable distance. Not far off stood, in an easy position, the Earl's handsome son and heir, Lord Adolphus Carlton, mallet in hand, explaining to pretty Alice Denham, the rector's daughter, what effect on the game his sister's stroke would have if correctly given. Kate Barton, the little golden-haired fairy, as she was called generally, is chatting merrily with the Honourable Eustace Carlton, a noble, aristocratic looking youth, with chestnut curls and the bright, flashing eyes of the Earl, his father, declaring with great animation that their side must win, while Maud Ashburnham, the physician's dark-haired daughter, a sparkling brunette, full of life and vivacity, announces to her partner, Alfred Arthur Denham, that her next stroke shall carry her through the last hoop, this will make her a rover, and she will then come to his assistance; and thus the game progressed, first in favor of one side and then the other, till at length a splendid stroke from the youthful Lady Eglentine's mallet, put her own and her partner's ball through the last wire arch, placing them in a triumphant position, amidst shouts of applause from their own side.

The game was now nearly over, for the bright orb of day had already sank behind the distant hills, and the silvery crescent of the summer's young moon had risen above the tops of the tall chestnuts and was shooting forth her rays of soft, pale light, rendering all objects shadowy and indistinct, while the gently deepening purple shades of eve, and the gray mists of twilight were fast closing in and around the happy group, hiding from further view, as it were, with a veil of soft, fleecy clouds, the family and fortunes of Arthur, Earl of Castlemere, and his beautiful Countess, Edith, the Lady of Vellenaux.

**THE END.**

Milton Keynes UK
Ingram Content Group UK Ltd.
UKHW042145281024
450365UK00010B/627